Titus Coan, Henry Martyn Field

Adventures in Patagonia

Titus Coan, Henry Martyn Field

Adventures in Patagonia

ISBN/EAN: 9783742886644

Manufactured in Europe, USA, Canada, Australia, Japa

Cover: Foto ©Andreas Hilbeck / pixelio.de

Manufactured and distributed by brebook publishing software (www.brebook.com)

Titus Coan, Henry Martyn Field

Adventures in Patagonia

ADVENTURES

IN

PATAGONIA

A

Missionary's Exploring Trip

BY THE
REV. TITUS COAN

WITH AN INTRODUCTION BY
REV. HENRY M. FIELD, D.D.

NEW YORK
DODD, MEAD & COMPANY
No. 755 Broadway
1880

COPYRIGHT, 1880, BY DODD, MEAD & COMPANY

CONTENTS

	PAGE
Introduction	i
Preface	7

CHAPTER I.
The Preparation... 9

CHAPTER II.
The Decision.. 21

CHAPTER III.
The Embarkation.. 30

CHAPTER IV
Arrival at our Landing Place........................... 46

CHAPTER V.
Visiting the Indian Camp............................... 65

CHAPTER VI.
A Squall.. 90

CHAPTER VII.
Chief Congo and his Clan.............................. 124

CONTENTS

CHAPTER VIII.
	PAGE
Arrival of the "Queen"	148

CHAPTER IX.
Sail ho!... 160

CHAPTER X.
Camp Life.. 190

CHAPTER XI.
Farewell to Patagonia...................................... 210

CHAPTER XII.
Life at the Falkland Islands............................... 221

CHAPTER XIII.
Homeward Bound... 254

CHAPTER XIV.
Mr. Darwin's Explorations.................................. 269

CHAPTER XV.
The Captive in Patagonia................................... 287

CHAPTER XVI.
The Story of Capt. Gardiner, R. N.......................... 291

CHAPTER XVII.
Later Efforts for Patagonia................................ 311

List of Writings Relating to Patagonia..................... 320

INTRODUCTION.

The writer of the following narrative is one of the most venerable of living missionaries, and a noble type of the "high caste" to which he belongs. With the strong religious conviction which comes from Puritan birth and training, with a faith that never doubts, and a zeal that inspires courage and devotion, he unites a practical turn of mind, a natural sagacity, and a quickness of adaptation to all vicissitudes of experience which may come to him in strange lands and among strange peoples—qualities which, combined, have made the American missionary a marked character in many parts of the world, and given him great success.

The Rev. Titus Coan is a native of New England, born in Killingworth, Conn., where his life began with the century, February 1st, 1801. He was the son of a farmer, and had no advantages but such as were afforded by the common schools. He developed a stalwart and rugged frame, and became noted for his physical strength. In manly sports he was an athlete, performing with ease the feat of lifting a barrel of flour to his shoulders. He joined a military company, in which his strength and courage gave him precedence, and he soon rose to be a captain. This military training was not lost upon him, and the endurance thus developed did him good service in the privations, hardships, and exposures of his after-life.

One could not live in Connecticut in those days without having his religious impressions and experiences. The famous evangelist, Asahel Nettleton, a native of Killingworth, was then setting New England aflame by his fervid eloquence. Whereever he went he was followed by crowds, to whom he preached with an earnestness and solemnity that filled them with awe. Young Coan was a cousin of Nettleton, and could not but be moved by the tide of religious feeling that swept over the country, though it was not till he had grown to manhood that he took the decided stand implied in making a "profession" of his faith. When religion takes hold of a strong character, it takes the stamp of the man, and stands out pronounced and positive. One who had been the athlete of his native town, foremost among his comrades, was not likely to be afraid of letting them see the new stand that he had taken. Prompt and bold in everything he did, no sooner had he come out on the Lord's side, than he "wheeled into line" with the precision of a soldier, and taking Christ for his Captain, marched in the van under his great Leader.

Hardly had he taken this stand, before his thoughts turned to the profession of the ministry. He was then living in Western New York, near Rochester, and the nearness of Auburn Seminary offered him a place for theological study. Preparing himself with such opportunities as he had (without the delay of going through college), he entered the Seminary in the fall of 1831. Looking forward to his future career, he had already decided to devote himself to the work of foreign missions, when the American Board (being assured by a sea captain lately returned from South America that a hopeful field might be found among the tribes of Patagonia) was looking around for a couple of intrepid soldiers of the Cross, to undertake an exploring expedition, and fixed upon young Coan, who had at once the physical strength and the fervent spirit. Reports were conflicting about the country and its people, and the expedition promised to be one of a good deal of adventure, if not of personal danger. It might be too much to say that the adventure and the danger were an attraction to the late captain of the militia but they certainly did not intimidate him. After due deliberation, taking counsel with his teachers, and with one whose voice might be more potent still, since she was to share his life and his fortunes in any quarter of the globe, he accepted the appointment, and with a fellow-student set out for the extreme point of the continent. The following pages contain the narrative of his adventures in Patagonia, which were certainly full enough of excitement and of danger to satisfy the most ardent spirit. A few months' experience of the wild country and its untamable inhabitants showed him that the field was not so promising as he had been told, and he returned to the United States for further orders He then married, and accompanied by his bride, set sail for the Hawaiian Islands, which through the voyages of whaling ships had become somewhat known to the American public. There was then no overland route, nor short cut across the Isthmus of Panama. They took the long course around Cape Horn, and were just six months on the voyage, when they came in sight of the beautiful islands which were to be their home for the rest of their days

Then began that long course of service which has few parallels in the annals of missionary life— few in the display of fidelity and devotion, "enduring hardship as a good soldier," and fewer still in its marvellous successes. Cast almost like a shipwrecked voyager on a distant shore, among a strange people, with whom at first he could only communicate through signs or by an interpreter, he set himself at once to master the language, and so quickly did he catch the words and inflections, that in three months he preached his first sermon to the natives in their own tongue. In his intercourse with this simple people, of whom he sought to gain the affection and confidence, he showed a tact which was his birthright as a son of New England. He had a great deal of mother wit and natural shrewdness and pleasant humor, which gave a charm to his conversation even with these untutored children of nature, while his overflowing kindness soon opened to him the door of every native's hut and heart. Desiring only to do them good, he tried to aid them in every way. He was a little of a doctor, knowing the remedies for the more common diseases, and, having a chest of medicines, prescribed for the poor people who were suffering. Often the natives stood in great numbers on the porch of his dwelling, with dusky arms outstretched, waiting for vaccination, or for his lancet to open a vein, that by bleeding they might be relieved of a burning fever. He even performed graver surgical operations. Those who had domestics troubles of any kind—wives who had shiftless husbands, or husbands who had termagant wives—alike sought the counsel of Father Coan, who was the general peacemaker. Thus he seemed to unite in himself the duties of preacher, pastor, and magistrate, and to be at once the teacher, guide, and friend of the whole population.

Nor were his labors confined to the spot where he lived. He made missionary tours to other parts of the island, now sailing in a canoe along the coast, and landing at the different places where he had made appointments to preach, and now climbing the slopes, which ascend in a series of ridges towards the mountains which make the centre of the island. In these journeys he encountered every sort of hardship. The tropical rains often came down in floods, converting in a few hours a rocky gorge into a foaming torrent, which no boat could cross and no swimmer could stem. But here his ready contrivance did not desert him. Calling to the natives on the other bank to throw him a rope, such as they make of the bark of the hibiscus, he seized it with his strong hands, and tying it around his body, was dragged across.

Thus the fame of this man of God spread abroad, and wherever he went the people "thronged him."

When he could not go to them they came to him. From all parts of the island they flocked to Hilo. "Whole villages gathered from many miles away, and made their homes near the mission house. Within the radius of a mile the little cabins clustered thick as they could stand. Hilo, the village of ten hundred, saw its population suddenly swelled to ten thousand, and here was held, literally, a camp meeting of two years. At any hour of the day or night a tap of the bell would bring together a congregation of from three to six thousand. Meetings for prayer and preaching were held daily."

Congregations so vast and so long continued have not often been assembled since Apostolic times, and the Spirit came down upon them as on the day of Pentecost. The preacher himself was thrilled by the scene, and catching an inspiration from the thousands of eager eyes and listening ears, felt lifted up with a strange power. "There was a fire in his bones." Were the congregation ever so large and tumultuous, it hushed at the sound of his voice. He said: "I would rise before the restless, noisy crowd and begin. It wasn't long before I felt that I had got hold of them. There seemed to be a chord of electricity binding them to me. I knew that I had them, that they would not go away. The Spirit would hush them by the truth till they would sob and cry 'What shall we do?' and the noise of the weeping would be so great that I could not go on."

As the fruit of these remarkable scenes a large part of the population abandoned heathenism, and professed to be converted to the Christian faith, insomuch, that when they came to be baptized, the good man was obliged to perform the sacred rite for them *en masse*. Seizing a brush like an *aspersarium*, and passing to and fro among the crowded rows of the candidates, he sprinkled them by scores and hundreds, pronouncing over them the name of the Father, the Son, and the Holy Ghost. Strange as it may seem to us, the service did not thereby lose any of its solemnity, but was rather more impressive from being done in this grand, majestic way, whereas on a smaller scale it might have lost by the endless repetition. By these immense additions the church at Hilo grew till it numbered over five thousand members, making the largest Protestant church in the world.

Mr. Coan and his wife remained on the islands thirty-five years before revisiting their native country. When they came back in 1870, they found another world than that which they had left. All things had become new. They had made their outward voyage in a small sailing vessel. They returned in a steamship. When they landed in San Francisco they had scarcely seen a railroad. Now they were whirled in fire-drawn cars up the mountains and over the plains, across the whole breadth of the continent. The fame of the missionary had gone before him, and wherever he came among the churches he was welcomed with an enthusiasm such as had not been manifested since the heroic Judson came back from Burmah, years before. When they visited New York they were guests in the house of the writer, where we were charmed alike by the intelligence, sprightliness, and animation of the veteran missionary, and the sweetness of her who had been his faithful companion during his long exile. It was then that, as we sat in the library, he talked freely, though very simply and modestly, of all the way in which God had led him. Among other things he related his early experiences in Patagonia, and it was perhaps in response to our suggestion and that of others that he prepared the narrative which follows.

They returned the following year, and when they reached the Islands were received by the natives with great demonstrations. Here was to be their home for the rest of their days. Two years after the wife and mother died, while the father still lives in his eightieth year—a hale and hearty old man, happy in the recollection of the past, happy in the good which he has done to the people to whom he has given his life, and happy in their tender and affectionate veneration. He cannot be expected to continue long. In a few more years he will be laid beside her whom he so much loved. Though they sleep far from their native land, it is not unmeet that they should be laid to rest in the island for which they had done so much; on those beautiful shores where the waters of the Pacific come rippling and murmuring up the beach. Nor will their memory depart. As long as the generation that knew them shall remain, the simple natives will often visit their graves, and recall their virtues with tears of love and gratitude.

H. M. F.

NEW YORK, March, 1880.

PREFACE.

THE following notes of a visit to Patagonia and the Falkland Islands are offered to the public in response to the call of many friends who desire to see the simple narrative in print.

These sketches of daily life at sea and among the wild savages of Patagonia were written for friends, and to assist personal recollections, and are now offered with diffidence simply as a plain record of facts and experiences.

The Supplement is added because the published narratives of visitors and missionary toilers among the Patagonian and Fuegian tribes have furnished new facts concerning those dark realms since the earlier part of the book was written. I have therefore taken the liberty to quote from the voyages of Admiral Fitzroy, Prof. Charles Darwin, Mr. Bourne, and from "The Story of Allen Gardiner," to all of which I am indebted for important information, as I am also to very many shipmasters, officers, and private friends, whose sympathy, unaffected courtesy, and generous aid were so liberally extended to my companion and to myself during that memorable year of our lives.

May Heaven's blessings rest upon them all in this life and throughout the future; and may the day be hastened when from every mountain-top and from the shining hills of heaven no "dark places shall be seen on earth" and no "habitations of cruelty"!

T. C.

HILO, HAWAII, 1879.

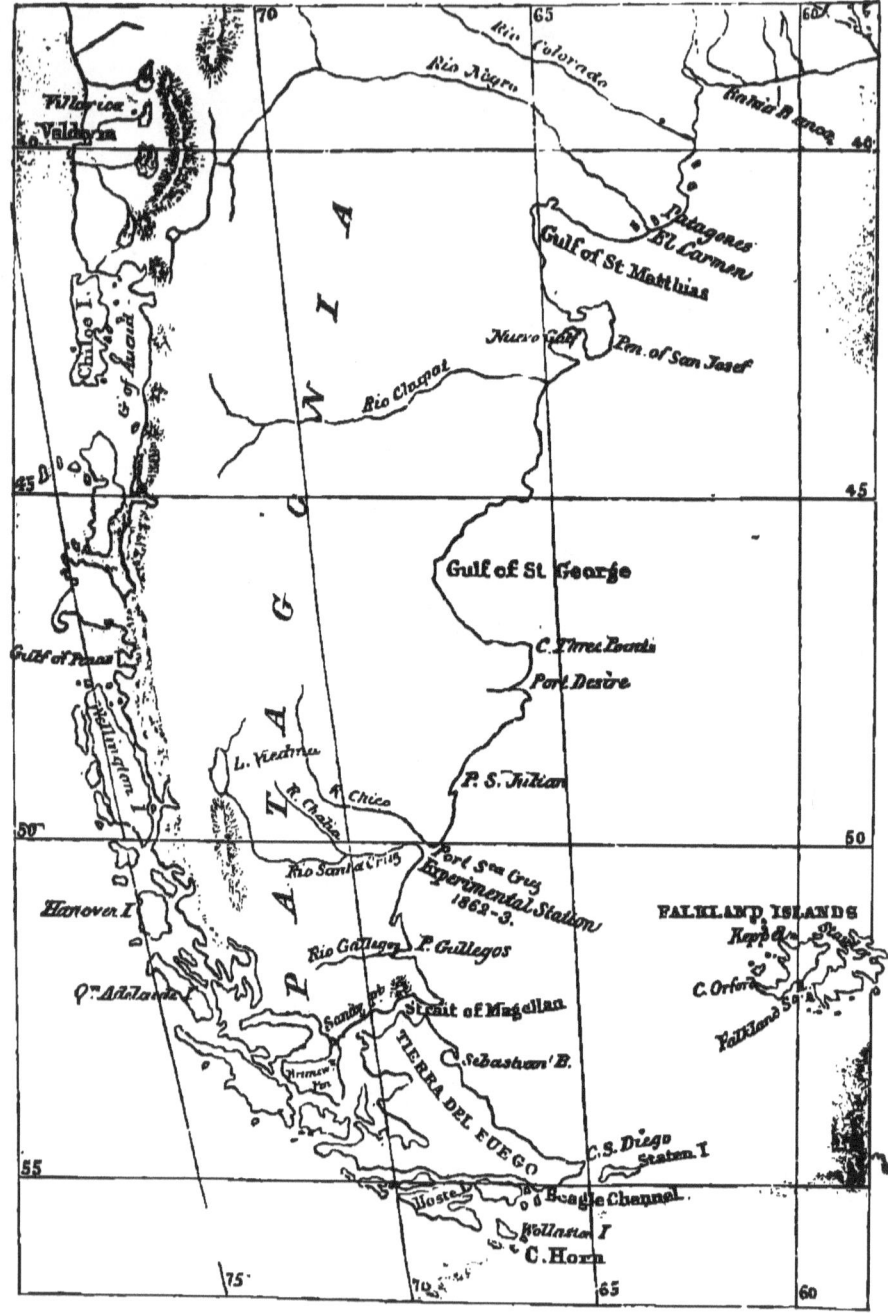

MISSION TO PATAGONIA.

CHAPTER I.

PREPARATION TO SEND A MISSSIONARY EXPLORING EXPEDITION TO PATAGONIA.

WHILE in the Theological Seminary at Auburn, N. Y., the following letter came to me one day in June, 1833:

"MISSIONARY ROOMS, BOSTON, June 19, 1833.
"MR. TITUS COAN,
   "*Theological Seminary, Auburn.*

"MY DEAR SIR: An exploring mission has been resolved upon by the Committee, Providence permitting, on the western coast of Patagonia. The vessel in which the mission must go, if it goes during the present year, is expected to sail on the last of July, and two missionaries can have a free passage. Two men ought by all means to go, and not one alone. One—Mr. Arms, of the Theological Seminary of Andover—has been engaged for the enterprise, and another is wanted. It occurred to us that perhaps you were the man. We received your testimonials, and made inquiries, and the result is that the question has been brought before the Committee, and they have unanimously appointed you a missionary of the Board, with special reference to this important expedition. Mr. Arms, the bearer of this letter, will explain to you the nature of the mission.

"The plan is, in brief, that two men, willing to endure hardship, be landed on the coast, at a place which is resorted to by sealing vessels, and spend a suitable time, probably a year or more, in travelling among the tribes of that coast; that they shall ascertain what can be done for them—where a mission had better be located, what should be the nature of the mission, etc.—and at the same time make arrangements for a mission, and then come home and report to the Committee. As this subject comes before you unawares, and you have but little time to reflect upon it, we do not ask you to decide now whether you will ultimately be a member of the Patagonian mission.

"The Committee will cheerfully leave this question to be determined at a future time, in view of Providential indications. The question now before you is, whether you will accompany Mr. Arms to the Patagonian coast and spend a couple of years, if necessary, among the Indian tribes of that coast? Of course you will both have to go unmarried. Mr. Arms leaves an intended wife behind him, and we understand that your circumstances are similar to his. The expedition now proposed to you is one full of privations; but it opens a prospect of bringing the Gospel to the minds and hearts of the poor degraded natives of Patagonia.

"Should you consent to go, you will come on to Boston by the 15th or 20th of July with all the necessary credentials for ordination, unless the Presbytery with which you are connected prefer to ordain you themselves, and can do it in season for you to be here at the time mentioned.

"I beg you to take this important subject into immediate and prayerful consideration. Let me hear from you as soon as possible. I earnestly hope you will go. If you do not, I see not how the mission can go during the present year.

"On your arrival in Boston we will confer with

you fully on the subject. The Lord be with you, my dear brother.

"Most truly yours,
"R. ANDERSON,
"Sec. A. B. C. F. M."

In connection with the foregoing earnest letter, Secretary Anderson sent me copies of a correspondence with Captain Benjamin Morrell, then in the city of New York. Captain Morrell had recently published a very attractive narrative of a cruise along the eastern coast of Patagonia, also through the Magellan Strait and up the Pacific coast as far as the island of Chiloe. In this journal he had given a glowing description of the harbors, the forests, the climate, soil, clover-meadows, and the numerous and peaceful inhabitants of the western coast of Patagonia. He had also taken occasion to hint that this coast would be a favorable field for missionary enterprise.

On reading this fascinating narrative, the Secretary opened a correspondence with Captain Morrell in order to elicit more definitely the important facts which would warrant sending an expedition with the view of establishing a mission on that coast.

The following is a copy of two letters of Captain Morrell to Secretary Anderson in answer to letters of inquiry from the Secretary.

"NEW YORK, Jan. 24, 1833.
"R. ANDERSON, Esq.

"DEAR SIR: Your favor of the 17th inst. is now before me, and it is with no ordinary degree of pleasure that I hasten to answer it.

"The interest you have taken in the temporal and eternal welfare of the now wretched and degraded natives of an unexplored region on the western coast of South America, between the Strait of Magellan and the Archipelago of Chiloe, has been highly gratifying to my feelings; and not the less so, I assure you, from your having derived the idea from the humble narrative I have just laid before the public. The harmless and inoffensive race of beings here alluded to are the migratory inhabitants of a country which is blessed with the most temperate climate, the richest soil, and the finest harbors on the face of the globe. It is true that at present these natives are more ignorant and debased than any other I have ever visited; but it is equally true that they are entirely free from many of the sensualities of the more enlightened, and are characterized by a mildness of disposition and a child-like simplicity of manners which in my humble opinion renders them fit subjects for missionary labor. They are ignorant of the simplest rudiments of agriculture, never dreaming that the luxuriant soil of their beautiful country would grant new favors to their slightest solicitation. Should heaven so far sanction the benevolent feelings which originated this correspondence as to enable your Society to establish a Christian mission among these children of nature, I have no hesitation in saying that a very few years would change their idle habits and wretched condition to those of comparative usefulness and happiness; while such a result would richly and amply reward me for all the time, labor, and personal hazards I have encountered in collecting the information I have published respecting them.

"In answering the series of questions you have done me the honor to propose, I shall beg leave to take them up in my own homely way and dispatch them in numerical order.

"The peninsula of Très Montes, in my opinion, is not the most eligible location on this coast for the establishment of a Protestant mission, on account of its proximity to the Catholic missions further north.

"For reasons which will presently appear, I would in preference designate the Guanaco Islands, or that section of the continent near which they lie, say lat. 47° south.

"The locating a similar establishment in any part of Magellan's Strait ought to depend on the success or failure of the project under consideration.

"I think that the Spanish States of South America would rather protect than seek to disturb a mission at the Guanaco Islands, because neither they nor the mother-country have ever conquered or asserted any claim to territories south of Chiloe.

"The natives I believe would treat the missionaries with the greatest kindness and respect.

"The Guanaco Islands, you are aware, are situated a short distance from the mainland, the northern island being in lat. 47° 31' S., lon. 75° 4' W. The most of these islands are of considerable extent, with spacious harbors between them. Their surface is low and level, partly covered with heavy timber, and on many of them there are beautiful plains of sufficient extent to raise produce the first season for several thousand natives; nothing more being required than to run a plough through a rich, mellow soil and cover the seed with the furrows. These plains are now covered with fine long grass, heavy clover, and extensive patches of celery, surrounded by lofty forests of various kinds of excellent ship timber.

"The waters abound with a great variety of the finest scale-fish, which may be taken in any quantities either with a seine or hook and line. Numerous kinds of shell-fish are found on the shores, as well as sea-otters and seals.

"The forests are teeming with a great variety of beautiful birds, and the mainland abounds in lions, guanacos, deer, hare, foxes, otter and many other valuable animals. Minerals, drugs, etc., are doubtless to be found in the interior.

"A few black cattle, sheep, goats, hogs, and poultry, turned out on those islands that were not to be immediately devoted to tillage, would increase and multiply and soon replenish them.

"The natives that inhabit the sea-coast are all travelling tribes, subsisting entirely on fish and such wild animals as they can procure, having no substitute for bread.

"Yours truly,
"BENJ. MORRELL."

"NEW YORK, Feb. 25, 1833."

"R. ANDERSON, Esq.

"DEAR SIR: Yours of the 21st inst. came duly to hand and is now before me.

"In reply to your first question, I can state from my own personal and frequent experience that the climate south of the equator in any given degree of latitude between 30° and 55° is neither so cold in winter nor so warm in summer as in the same degrees of N. lat. In lat. 47°, there is seldom any snow in the valleys. The storms are not more frequent nor more severe than in New England.

"The number of natives between lat. 47° and 50° I take to be about 20,000. They sojourn in one place till they have exhausted the shell-fish, and then remove to another. They have no tame animals except dogs. Interpreters can be obtained at Chiloe who understand their language and will translate it into Spanish.

"The natives are honest and will respect private property. The coast can be traversed with safety in canoes; but to penetrate into the interior horses will be necessary, which must be taken from the United States.

"In closing this hasty communication I beg leave to express the satisfaction I feel in your having taken this interesting subject into consideration, and trust that your exertions in behalf of the benighted heathen will meet a due reward. Under such a hope, I subscribe myself,

     "Yours truly,
       "BENJ. MORRELL."

It will be seen that these letters of Captain Morrell embrace answers to many specific questions addressed to him by the Secretary of the American Board of Commissioners for Foreign Missions.

In order to increase information on the subject which now engaged the earnest attention of the Prudential Committee of the Board, the Secretary addressed a letter of inquiry to Silas E. Burrows, Esq., of New York City, as Mr. Burrows was the owner of several vessels engaged in sealing along the coasts of Patagonia and among the islands of Tierra del Fuego, and as Captain Morrell had been engaged in his service. Mr. Burrows had also been on the Pacific coast as far as Chili, and it was hoped that he might know something of the country and tribes described by Captain Morrell. This letter Mr. Burrows answered promptly, and with characteristic enthusiasm; and although he was unable to add any information to that of his

Captain, yet he fully endorsed his high character and assured the Secretary that the Missionary Board might place implicit confidence in his statements.

Mr. Burrows furthermore stated that he was then fitting out a sealing schooner, the Mary Jane, to sail from New York City in July, and that he would be most happy to give a free passage in said schooner to two young gentlemen who might desire to explore on the western coast of Patagonia. He also stated that he would instruct the master of the Mary Jane, Captain William Clift, to look well to the missionaries, to land them at any points on the coast where they desired to explore, and to return them to the United States at the end of the voyage.

Up to this point all things looked favorable, and the voice of Providence seemed to say, "*Go forward.*" With these letters and testimonials Mr. Arms was sent by the Committee from Boston to Auburn, to converse with me, and to urge, if necessary, my acceptance of the appointment as an exploring missionary to Patagonia.

I had just returned from Rochester, where I had supplied the pulpit of one of the pastors during vacation. About nine o'clock in the morning these communications were put into my hands for consideration. I was then entering on my last term in the Theological Seminary. At its close I was engaged to marry Miss Fidelia Church, and I hoped to go with her as a missionary to some foreign land. We had been betrothed for years, and this call, if accepted, would throw a cloud over the prospects of our union for a long time at least, perhaps forever.

But the question must be met, and met *immediately*. It was now late in June, and the vessel bound to Patagonia was to sail before the close of July; and if I failed, the expedition must fail for that year at least, as it was deemed impossible to find another man to take the place in due season.

CHAPTER II.

THE DECISION.

I CALLED on Dr. Richards, President of the Seminary, put the papers into his hands, and requested him to confer with Drs. Perrine and Mills, the other members of the Faculty, and give me advice.

The Professors met by call, and soon the venerable Dr. Richards, with brimming eyes, reported that, as the voice of God seemed to call me to this service, they could not object to my going; that, while they did not feel at liberty to give me positive advice, they approved of the proposed Patagonian mission, and that, should I decide to go, their prayers should go with me, and that I should have an honorable release from the further duties of the Seminary.

Thus another door was opened and another voice seemed to say, "*Go.*"

News of this call spread quickly through the Seminary, and many of the students rushed to my room to inquire. Some with tears entreated me not to go, with language like this: "The Patagonians are ferocious cannibals; they will kill and eat you. You have no right to throw away your life, as you are now just prepared to labor in the vineyard."

Others said, "*Go, brother;* the Lord will go with you, and nothing shall harm you; for Jesus has said, 'Lo, I am with you alway.'" As I was then busy in preparing to leave Auburn, the brethren were requested to come to my room at 5 P.M., when I would be ready and happy to see all who would do me the favor to call. During that hour the room was crowded, conversation was free, prayer was offered, and tearful farewells and benedictions uttered.

At nine o'clock of the evening of the day on which the Boston letters came to hand the stage for Rochester was before the Seminary door, and I took my seat for the night. Early the next morning I was in Rochester, where I had left my espoused but a few days before.

She was at breakfast when I entered her house. After salutations I took breakfast with the family; then came morning prayers, during all which time nothing had been said as to why I had returned so soon to Rochester. All was mystery to Miss Church and her friends.

After prayers we retired to a separate room, and I, without a word of explanation, put Dr. Anderson's letter into her hands. As she read, her emotion deepened, her tears flowed. What a change of situation! What an uprooting of fondly and long cherished hopes! For seven years we had waited, and now only three or four months remained before our nuptials were to be celebrated, and we were to go forth into some foreign field, to toil, to suffer, and to rejoice together in the vineyard of our Master. For a minute she was dumb. The struggle was intense. Soon, however, faith gained the victory. That full consecration which, long before, she had made to her Master and Lord assumed its power; her soul rose from the stern conflict of emotion—of hope deferred, perhaps slain. She took my hand and said, "*My dear, you must go.*"

This settled the question. There was no looking back. Another door was opened, and again the voice seemed to say, "*Go forward.*"

Henceforth it was preparation in earnest. I spent a few days in visiting friends in Western New York with Miss Church; then came a tender farewell, she returning to Rochester, while I hastened on to Boston. There I met Mr. Arms, my companion in the enterprise; and on Sunday evening, July 28th, 1833, we were ordained in Park Street Church. On the 29th we received our instructions for the Patagonian expedition from the Prudential Committee of the A. B. C. F. M., in the house of the venerable chairman, the Hon. S. Hubbard.

All things being now ready, we took passage for New York to embark for Patagonia.

In order to assist us in any further necessary preparations, Mr. Henry Hill, Treasurer of the Missionary Board, accompanied us to New York. He also furnished us with ample letters of credit on banking houses in Valparaiso and London, and the Secretary of the Board gave us letters of introduction to the commodore commanding the U. S. squadron on the Pacific station.

This was precautionary, in case we should find it necessary to reach Valparaiso in order to obtain passage to the United States, and perhaps *via* England or France.

On our arrival in New York we were met by the Rev. David Green, one of the secretaries of the American Board, who had just returned from a visit to the Cherokee Mission; also by the Hon. Pelatiah Perit, a corporate member of the Board; by Mr. Silas E. Burrows, owner of the Mary Jane and patron of the Patagonian mission; by Captain William Clift, of Mystic, Connecticut, the Master of the Mary Jane; and by many others of the friends and patrons of Christian missions.

And now came a shock of disappointment. Captain Clift assured us that the officers of the Board had been misled by the recently published book of Captain Morrell. He denied the statements as to the fine climate, the beautiful lands, the luxuriant meadows of clover, the considerable number of the inhabitants, their quiet habits and their amiable disposition.

In confirmation of his denial he stated that he had sailed up and down the whole western coast of Patagonia several times; had seen the bays, channels, islands, the mainland, and the natives; that he had sealed from the western entrance of Magellan's Strait to the island of Chiloe, and that the description of that coast by Captain Morrell was far from being correct. Captain Clift described the coast as broken, mountainous, wild, and the climate as often stormy. The ravines, headlands, cliffs, spurs, and precipitous sea-walls, he said, rendered travelling by land along the shore impossible, and by sea in a boat very difficult and dangerous.

"As for the inhabitants," said Captain Clift, "they amount to only a few scores, and these are the most wretched and squalid creatures I have ever seen in human form: small in size, nearly naked, having only the protection of a piece of seal-skin hung over the windward shoulder, and turning this from side to side as their canoes tacked or the wind changed. They live most of the time in canoes, paddling from rock to rock, and subsisting on shell-fish, seals, and dead whales which sometimes drift on shore." He added that there were no villages, or settlements of Indian tribes, along that whole coast; that the natives had no idea of agriculture, and that the land was unfit for tillage; in short, that it was the most dreary and inhospitable coast imaginable.

These statements were corroborated by the testimony of a number of masters, officers, and sailors who had been up and down that coast on sealing expeditions; and the testimony of Captain King, of the British navy, who once surveyed that coast, was substantially the same.

Furthermore, Captain Clift said that on the

present voyage he should not visit that coast at all; that he would enter the Strait of Magellan, and seal among the lagoons, inlets, channels, rocks, and numerous islets of Tierra del Fuego; that to take the missionaries to the west coast of Patagonia would change the whole plan of his voyage, and probably make it an entire failure; and that to land us where we were instructed to go, to look after us along that coast, and to pledge himself to take us off and return us to the United States when our explorations were ended, was out of the question. He also said that to land and leave us there, without care or means of escape, would be but to abandon us to a cruel death.

All this put a new and dark aspect on the Patagonian mission. What could be done? Must we go back to Boston? Must we acknowledge failure, return our instructions, and seek another field of labor?

This seemed like "putting the hand to the plough and looking back." We looked at one another, but all was blank. We looked to the Lord for guidance, and in half an hour the problem was solved.

Captain Clift said, "Gentlemen, if you wish to

go to *Eastern Patagonia*, I will take you into the Strait of Magellan and land you on the north shore, among the Horse Indians, and then pursue my voyage, which may be one or two years. My object is to fill my vessel with seal-skins, whether the time be longer or shorter. Should you be on the shore, where I can reach you, when I return, I will take you home, but more than this I cannot promise."

Our instructions from the Prudential Committee had cautioned us to avoid, if possible, getting among the Eastern Patagonians, as they were reputed to be fierce savages of gigantic size, and cannibals withal.

Captain Clift said, " They are hard fellows ; but vessels passing through the Strait sometimes trade with them unharmed."

The question was now reduced to this: to go among the Eastern Patagonians, under the conditions above stated, or to abandon the mission for the present at least, if not altogether.

A council of the members and friends of the American Board then present in New York was held. After prayer and due consultation, the following question was put to the young missionaries: " Are you willing, in view of all the circumstances and conditions of the case, to go to Eastern Patagonia?" The reply was, promptly, "Yes."

The meeting then voted unanimously to approve of our desire to embark on this untried enterprise.

After renewed prayers, in which the missionaries and the cause were tenderly commended to the grace of God, the meeting was dissolved, and the missionaries at once set about finishing their preparations for sailing from New York.

CHAPTER III.

THE EMBARKATION.

HAVING completed our outfit, written our last letters to distant correspondents, and bidden adieu to many kind and faithful friends in New York, we went on board the little schooner Mary Jane on the 16th of August, 1833, and sailed for one of "the ends of the earth."

From my journal of our voyage to Patagonia I make extracts:

Schooner Mary Jane, off Sandy Hook, Aug. 16, 1833.—By the good hand of God, our voyage to the far South is now commenced. We have bidden smiling and weeping friends farewell. The city, with its turrets and towers and lofty spires, has faded in the distance. Its busy hum is hushed. With favoring breeze and pilot at the helm, our little bark has sped down the channel, and now the great ocean opens on our sight. The sun is setting behind the western hills of my beloved country. The wind has died away. A placid calmness rests on the deep.

Captain Clift calls all hands, exhorts them to observe the rules of morality, and to obey orders *promptly* and *cheerfully*. He then invited one of us to offer up prayer to Almighty God.

Aug. 17. We slept—and awaked. But the city, the islands, the Bay, the headlands, the continent with all its distant hills, have disappeared like a "vision of the night" All is ocean around and under us, and our little cockle-shell is ploughing a white foaming furrow along the bosom of the deep.

On the 18th we had a heavy gale. Our light shallop danced and leaped and staggered, and plunged like a mermaid into the foaming billows, and like a duck or a swan received the spray and the leaping waves upon her deck. We were in the Gulf-stream, and were severely handled for several days, shipping heavy seas, but coming out well.

Sept. 7—lat. 34° 11' N., lon. 29° 12' W. We have had both stormy and fair weather; have sighted one ship and one brig, but were not able to speak to them. We have religious services on board when the weather is good, and a part of the crew seem attentive and thoughtful. Some retire to quiet places on deck to read the Bible and religious books and tracts, and to converse. Others are hard and heathenish. A few seem resolved to reform and lead new lives.

Our sympathies are much moved for a young sailor whose name is Charles Palmer, of N. Y. City. He says that he is a member of Dr. Phillips' church, of N. Y., but that becoming somewhat thoughtless he shipped on board the Mary Jane without the consent of his parents. For this he is now very sorry, as he is often attacked with fearful cramps and convulsions, attended with delirium. Mr. Arms, having studied medicine, administers anti-spasmodics and sedatives; and during these attacks I give up my berth to him, and sleep on the transom. He seems grateful for these cares.

Sept. 22. On ascending to the deck this morning we were surprised to find our little vessel among the Cape de Verde Islands, and close under the lee of the island Brava. A noble brig lay at anchor in the bay, floating the "stars and stripes." Soon a boat came alongside, when we learned that the vessel was the Susan Elizabeth, Captain Davis, of Boston, bound to Rio de Janeiro. This was the first vessel we had spoken, though we had sighted five sails on our way. We glided slowly away from the Cape de Verdes without anchoring or landing, and soon lost sight of land.

Oct. 6. Captain Clift and Mr. Burrows, the mate, hunted the heavens and the sea to-day for our latitude, but could find none. They found 20° of longitude. For 50 days we have been striving hard to *consume* our latitude, and it has just left us, but we shall struggle again to gain more than we have lost. We wish to make 52° from the great Southern Hemisphere. We have glided smoothly over the equator without feeling a jar, and, better still, that slimy old rascal, Neptune, has not boarded us with his razor and slush-pot and brush ; nor has Bacchus intruded with bottle and song and revelry. May these sea-monsters sink forever in the deep!

Oct. 9—lat. 6° S. For 54 days we have been pursuing the sun as he has been moving south on his blazing car. To-day we have overtaken him, and he looks down upon us from the zenith of his glory, flooding us with his vertical rays. Now we could truly say :

"Your form no darkling shadow throws
Across the vessel's deck."

We shall now run south of the sun for a long time, and may often long for his nearer visits.

How our little planet swings and changes position! The great Northern Hemisphere, with all its golden constellations, seems to be dipping, while the Southern rises and hangs out its shining lamps to guide our pathway over the dark abyss of waters.

The Southern Cross, also, rises higher and higher to remind us of the Sacrifice and of our great errand into the wild and dreary realms of the South.

Oct. 12—lat. 14° 15' S. Our speed is now 200 miles a day. One of the Magellan clouds is in full view, hanging about 10 degrees above the horizon. The appearance of this nebula is like that of the galaxy, and it is, no doubt, formed by the blended rays of unnumbered stars.

Our seasons are now all reversed. We are in the midst of an opening spring, while the blasts of autumn are sweeping over the North. It seems odd to look north for the sun, and to see our tiny shadows fall southward.

Oct. 15. Land ho! At daylight our good captain awoke us to see the island of Trinidad, in lat. 20° 28' S. Before sunrise we also made the islands of Martin Vas, four in number, lying 9 leagues east of Trinidad.

These islets are rough, rocky heaps of volcanic

products rising abruptly from the ocean to the height of several hundred feet, sterile and uninhabited except by a few goats and many seabirds. We did not land, and before noon all *terra firma* had sunk below the horizon.

Oct. 23—lat. 34° 3' S. We had a rousing gale on the 20th, with drenching rain and boisterous sea. Since then we have had variable weather, but have run rapidly on our course.

Birds of the "south seas" gather thick about us. The lively little stormy-petrel, called by sailors " Mother Cary's Chickens," and the Cape pigeons are very numerous and sportive. The soaring mollemoke (*Procellaria glacialis*) and the proud albatross (*Diomedia exulans*) sail gracefully above and around us, often lighting and dancing on the rolling waves. The albatross is very large, often measuring from 12 to 13 feet from tip to tip of his outspread wings.

On the 25th and 26th we were visited by a storm of wind, rain, and thunder more terrible than any that we had experienced. The night was dark, the rain poured in torrents, the tempest howled through the strained rigging, and ever and anon the thunderbolts from the black and swirling clouds came with a crash which seemed to rend the heavens, causing the "poor sailors to stand amazed and quiver," while the blazing lightning seemed to set the clouds on fire and revealed the angry billows of the ocean rolling in sublime majesty and threatening to swallow up our bark with all on board.

How strikingly we were reminded of the sublime language of the royal psalmist: "The Lord sitteth king upon the floods. The voice of the Lord is upon the waters; the God of glory thundereth; the Lord is upon many waters"!

On the 27th the storm had subsided, and the day was quiet. We saw whales, porpoises, and sea-fowls, great and small, in abundance. On the 28th almost a dead calm attended us, and multitudes of birds gathered around us. By feeding them we drew a large family within a fathom of our vessel. There was something social and domestic in the sight of this brood, and it afforded us no little amusement to see the dexterity with which they dived after pieces of meat thrown to them.

Oct. 31. After another gale more severe than any I have hitherto recorded on this voyage, we are able again to use our pens to tell of "the works of the Lord and his wonders in the deep."

THE EMBARKATION.

During the night of the 28th, in lat. 40° S., long. 53° W., the wind returned in fresh strength and continued to increase until morning, when it proved to be a terrific pampéro, blowing directly from the great pampas of S. America. Amidst the roar of the wind the stern command of the captain was heard, "All hands ahoy!" and in two minutes all hands were on deck making everything as secure as possible.

All the sails were furled, except the head of the foresail, just enough to make the vessel feel the helm.

Under this small piece of canvas the vessel was put before the wind, which blew from the SW., and made to stand to the NE., which was going directly back over the ground we had passed. Soon the gale increased into a fearful hurricane, and the angry waves assumed a more threatening aspect, continually boarding us from every quarter and threatening to engulf us.

Scudding now became unsafe, as the danger of broaching to, upsetting, and sinking was imminent.

For hours no man on board but the captain dared touch the helm. The chief mate was a man of iron frame, but he shrank from the helm in dismay, and there stood the brave master—an excellent seaman—breasting the roaring tempest and fighting the foaming billows until his strength was nearly exhausted, when, with admirable skill and resolution, he succeeded in "heaving to" the drenched and laboring bark. The day was dark and fearful, the wind increasing every hour. The conflict of the elements exceeded anything we had ever seen. The roar of the winds, the towering of the waves, the reeling and creaking and trembling of the vessel, the giving way of spars and rigging, the breaking of railings and bulwarks, and the hoarse voice of command from the officers, all bespoke a scene of confusion, of awe, and of peril which none can understand but those who have witnessed a tempest at sea. All day long on the 29th the wind seemed to increase in strength and fury, and the waves rolled in sublime grandeur. Every succeeding billow as it approached our little bark looked as if it must go over us, but, coming under the bows and passing away at the stern, it lifted us upon its crest, where for a moment our vessel quivered, as if sensitive to fear, and then plunged down an angle of some 20 degrees into the deep valley—the "trough of the sea"—in which her topmasts could hardly have been seen from the valley beyond the next billow.

So long as these mountain waves were regular there was little danger; it was a sight of grace and beauty to see the majestic wave as it came under the vessel, lifting her up some 20 to 30 feet, holding her for a few seconds on its foaming crest, sprinkling her with a white feathery spray as with snowflakes, and then letting her down its sloping side into the deep valley below. It seemed somewhat like marine *coasting*, and indeed the motion was not unpleasant.

But ever and anon came a fierce, foaming billow, towering high and roaring as if to devour us. This would sometimes "comb over" and break, striking on the stern, on the bow, amidships, on our quarters, or along the whole length of the ship's sides, sweeping our decks from "stem to stern," dashing down the companion-way, drenching the cabin, setting furniture afloat in wild confusion, and soaking our berths, our clothing, our books and papers, and seeming, for the time being, to have full control of the ship, the cargo, and the crew. These were fearful breaches, and it often seemed as if all was lost. But it was wonderful to see our little shallop rise like a sea-gull from such a crashing and drenching flood, shake herself from the foam which filled her scuppers and poured in cataracts over her sides, and like a storm-bird adjust herself for another charge of her marine assailant.

During most of the time the sailors were holding on to the standing rigging with desperate grasp. No table was laid, and no one ate except by snatches.

This was a wind-storm from the great Buenos Ayres pampas, or prairies. There was no rain, nor thunder and lightning, and yet the sun was invisible by day and the stars by night, and no observations could be taken to determine our latitude and longitude until the storm was over. The obscuration of the heavenly bodies arose from the immense clouds of spray raised by the tempest, which filled the atmosphere to a great height and fell like a dense Scotch mist upon our decks. So thick was this spray that at times we could not see the bowsprit from the main deck, and a sailor at a few yards' distance looked more like Hamlet's ghost than like a man.

But all things in nature are governed by the law of compensation, and so it is with the laws of storms. Strong winds can raise the ocean waves to a certain height, after which they have no power to elevate; but, on the contrary, as the wind increases it can only depress the billows by its great pressure, and by *uncapping*, so to speak, the waves and lifting their crested foam into the atmosphere in the form of spray, in which the sun in his brightness paints rainbows and makes all the prismatic tints quiver and dance in aërial beauty.

But our sympathies were greatly moved for the master, the officers, and the whole crew during this terrific tempest. Everything alow and aloft was thoroughly drenched with the boarding waves or with the thick, cold mist. We had no chance for drying by night or day, and were also unable to cook or to get hot food; so that all of us were shivering and chilled with cold. The sight of the vessel and of all on board was dreary enough; but if the poet be correct,

" The darkest day, live till to-morrow, will have passed away;"

and so this storm ended, and we said with joy: " He maketh the storm a calm, so that the waves thereof are still. Then are they glad because they are quiet."

Captain Clift labored with amazing energy,

thorough nautical skill, and untired patience and care to save our ship and all on board from a grave in the deep; and his officers and crew were prompt and ready to obey orders. The captain and the officers all say that they have never before passed through such an awful tempest.

This last day of October is one of gladness. All are engaged in repairing the damages to the vessel, in drying clothing, and enjoying the warm sunshine.

Nov. 1. We are far from our course, having sailed and drifted many miles northwardly during the storm.

Charles Palmer, the sailor heretofore mentioned as afflicted with convulsions, had a severe attack last night, and was brought into the cabin, where we cared for him.

Nov. 8—lat. 48° S., lon. 65° 14′ W. At 10 A.M. the cry "Land ho!" rang from all parts of the vessel. The low, sandy shores of Eastern Patagonia near Cape Blanco are in full view about thirty miles to the westward. The day is delightful; the sky unclouded, the air soft and bland, the rays of the sun mild and grateful, all giving indications of the vernal season. But we see no fields smiling under the hand of the husbandman; no gardens and orchards dressed in the blooming beauties of spring; no harbors adorned with the waving flags of commerce; no cities lifting their towers against the sky; no peaceful villages and dainty hamlets sprinkling the extended plains; no glittering church-spires pointing the weary pilgrim to "a better country." Art and science have never shed their kindly influences over this benighted land; nor has the "Light of Life" yet dawned upon it. Here the fierce savage has roamed from age to age, tearing the flesh and drinking the blood of his prey. Generation after generation has gone down to the shades of death without a beam of light to cheer the dark valley, or a "morning star" to give promise of "an eternal day."

Night.—A strong westerly breeze sets us eastward, and we have lost sight of the land.

Nov. 10. We have had divine service on board to-day, for the last time probably. Our next Sabbath we expect to spend among the Patagonian savages.

We have enjoyed religious worship on the Lord's day when it has been fine weather during the voyage, and our little congregation is dear to us. Some of the crew express faith in Christ, and others have appeared sober-minded and impressible under the sound of the Gospel.

Nov. 11. At 5 P.M. we made Cape Virgin on the north bank of the entrance to Magellan Strait, bearing due west and distant about eighteen miles.

Nov. 12. Arose this morning and found the Mary Jane within the Strait, beating against a strong head-wind. At noon we passed the first "narrows," but at 5 P.M. we were obliged to anchor on account of a strong head-wind and current. As our vessel dragged fast, the anchor was taken up, when one of the flukes was found broken off, and we were in peril of drifting on shore. Sail was instantly made, and our vessel ran back through the narrows till a new anchorage was found, when another anchor was let go, which held the ship.

Captain Clift reported the broken anchor as a new one purchased in New York. On examination it was found that a flaw in the fluke had been filled with putty and concealed with paint! Such a flaw has its moral.

The land on each side of the Strait is thus far low and gently undulating, with here and there a hill of little height. The beach is white sand. As we sailed along, the savages on either side raised a great smoke in many places. This is a common signal on descrying a vessel approaching their coast.

Nov. 13. We lay at anchor all day on account of a fierce westerly wind. As the tide fell, Captain Clift found it necessary to drop off into deeper water. Much difficulty was encountered in finding good holding ground, and we were all apprehensive of being driven out again into the open Atlantic. At length, however, good anchorage was found, and our bark rides safely.

CHAPTER IV.

ARRIVAL AT OUR LANDING-PLACE.

Nov. 14. On awaking this morning we found the Mary Jane quietly anchored in Gregory's Bay, some seventy miles from the entrance of the Strait.

Thus our voyage of just ninety days is ended, and the land for which we sailed is before us. We look out upon a beach of white sand, upon sand-cliffs, sand-dunes, the grassy pampas and distant snow-crowned hills; but neither man nor beast nor human habitation is visible: all is drear solitude.

Captain Clift, with true kindness, offered to remain for a day or two to assist us in finding Indians, and to give us a home on board his vessel until we could get quarters among the savages.

Accordingly we landed early in the morning upon a beautiful beach, and, mounting a steep bank some fifty feet high, we found dry grass and

ARRIVAL AT OUR LANDING-PLACE. 47

a small clump of thorny bushes resembling the barberry, with a yellow blossom. With these we made a smoke as a signal to raise the savages. Not succeeding, we returned before noon to the vessel, and at 1 P.M. we landed again with the Captain, determined to travel back into the country till we should find some human beings. Taking one of the Indian trails, of which we saw many, we pursued our way over hills and vales, often coming upon places where the savages had encamped, and which were thickly strewn with the bones of animals consumed by them—bones chiefly of the guanaco, a variety of the lama.

In one instance we saw two huge vertebræ of a whale's spine, far inland. The tracks of horses, dogs, and guanacos were visible everywhere.

One of the latter animals we descried feeding alone in a meadow, but on seeing us he went like an antelope over the ground, and was soon out of sight. We saw several large fowls, among which was the thievish rook, the curlew, and the upland goose. Several small birds also flitted around us, cheering us with their sweet warbling.

The hills over which we passed were of a dark sandy soil, very light, free from stones, and covered with grass. The meadows were a rich alluvium covered with very thick grass, which grows in spontaneous profusion.

As the old tore (dry grass) still remained in abundance, we found it easy to raise a great smoke to arouse the savages. But on and on we went with rapid speed, as we were all very anxious to find Indians before night: the Captain because he wished to sail as soon as possible, and we because we felt the importance of meeting the natives before the Mary Jane should leave. We entered a little ravine, at the head of which we found a rill of pure water, where we slaked our great thirst. Soon after we found a larger stream running through a grassy meadow.

How far we travelled we know not, but our march was rapid because we were all urged on by our earnest desires to find inhabitants that day. Probably we walked from seven to ten miles towards the high lands north of us. But the descending sun and our weary limbs called for retreat; so back we sped to the beach, where we arrived at nightfall, hungry, thirsty, weary, and disappointed.

Nov. 15. Early this morning, Captain Clift in company with Mr. Arms set out again in search of Indians, while I remained on board to attend to some business preparatory to leaving the vessel.

After noon we descried one savage on the beach, and shortly after he was joined by three more, all mounted on horseback and attended by more than twenty dogs. In a little time Mr. Arms and the Captain appeared on the bank above the beach, when a boat was sent from the schooner to bring them on board. Three of the savages came off with them, one of whom is a son of an aged chief whom they call *el capata le grande*, the grand captain. The young man is of more than middling size, firmly built, of an open countenance, and, for a savage, of modest and pleasant manners. He can speak a few words in English and more in Spanish. By signs and a little Spanish we signified to him that we wished him to furnish us with two horses and be our guide to the Indian camp among the northern hills, where we could spend the night, and return with him to the shore in the morning.

This we were very anxious to do, that we might learn what we could about Patagonian life before the Mary Jane leaves us. The young chief seemed to understand and to consent to our desires. So we took him on shore, where he selected two horses for us, and, mounting his own, we set off on full gallop, leaving three Indians and one horse on the shore. After riding rapidly for four or five miles, our guide dismounted, drew out two pebbles from his skin pouch, struck fire and kindled the dry grass around us. This soon made a dense smoke, which was the signal for the other savages of his clan to come down.

He then waited a while, looking earnestly to the hills, but we as earnestly beckoned him to remount his horse and ride on. He obeyed, and we rushed over another plain, when he dismounted again, made another great smoke, and waited again for the Indians.

We pressed him once more to go on, as night was approaching and we feared we should not reach the lodge that day. So on we galloped, but shortly we descried dark forms coming down the side of the mountain from a pass among the hills, one or two miles distant. Then another and another squad followed, while we rode on to meet them. The first detachment came up like a whirlwind, their long, coarse black hair streaming and their rough skin mantles flapping in the wind, while all were shouting in savage glee. The ground shook under the rush of their horses,

ARRIVAL AT OUR LANDING-PLACE.

and the atmosphere was clouded with dust. They surrounded us; they yelled and grinned; they were as noisy as a flock of loons, and as active as a swarm of bees. They talked with our guide; they tried to talk with us; they examined and counted our garments; they opened our vests, felt in our pockets, pulled up our trousers and thrust their hands into our boots. This was rough courtesy and a savage reception.

Probably all this examination was to ascertain whether we had arms or tobacco. The former would have excited suspicion; the latter aroused their cupidity.

They were large, strong, and bold men, quite independent in their bearing, and perfectly conscious that they were "masters of the situation." They were dark and filthy, ignorant and brutal in the last degree; and yet each man was a king in his own estimation, and their country was the greatest, the richest, and the best in the world. It had never been conquered, and these proud men were lords who knew no masters.

They laughed, showing splendid rows of white teeth, and in five minutes the interview ended. Every man put spurs to his horse, and, with yells and an uproarious shout, the whole band, of about twenty, rushed toward the Strait, leaving a long cloud of dust behind them.

Our guide wished to turn back and go with them to the shore, but we still urged him to proceed to the camp. This he did reluctantly, often lingering, dismounting, and showing a desire to return. We met a few more straggling companies of savages, and when the last came up it was impossible to press him forward any longer. We judged ourselves to be ten or twelve miles from the sea, with no signs of an Indian camp in sight. So when our guide turned his horse's head toward the shore, we had no alternative, and we wheeled also. This was near sundown. We gave our coursers the rein and followed our savage friends without stopping to think, to wink, or to breathe.

At 10 P.M. we were back on the beach, where we found the companies we had met encamped in the open air for the night. We hailed our vessel, but had no response. She was anchored more than half a mile from the shore; her lights were extinguished, her crew asleep, and we were to spend our first night on shore with these wild people without shelter or supper. About forty savages were scattered around, some sleeping and snoring, some talking in unknown gutturals, some grunting, and some hunting small game in the hair of their dogs, of which about a hundred were present, while the horses were tethered around with raw-hide thongs. A small clump of thorn-bushes near the beach had supplied the savages with a few fagots with which they had kindled a flickering fire, which furnished just light enough to render the darkness and the dark visages visible. Around these smoking fagots sat a number of Indians trying to warm in the smoke and ashes a few small pieces of dirty guanaco meat, of which they gave Mr. Arms and myself each a morsel about the size of one's finger. This was our supper. But we were weary and hungry, and so without scruple, "asking no questions," we ate our morsels with thankfulness. This was a foretaste of Patagonian life. The Indians also gave us a little water from a skin bottle, or bag such as the old patriarchs used, and this was a kind of prelibation of the blessings in store for us in this wild land.

After our repast and our thanksgiving, our guide spread a skin for us to sleep on, and when we lay down he tried to cover us with a small, thin, and not very clean blanket. It was kind in him, and we appreciated the service; for it was a cold night and the dew was heavy, so that we awoke in the morning wet and chilled. But we slept peacefully and without fear, and awoke thankful for the protecting care of Israel's Shepherd.

Nov. 16. The morning is bright and cool. The sun of our northern home shines upon us, but all our surroundings are strange and weird. The Captain sent his boat early, and we went on board, taking with us the old chief before mentioned, his son our guide and one other Indian. All these seemed to be prominent men of the tribe and our object in taking them on board was to make arrangements with them for living and travelling with them in Patagonia until our mission to their country should be accomplished.

Through seamen who have visited the Strait and seen numbers of this tribe of savages, we learn that a chief whom the sailors called Maria and dubbed the Queen was somewhere in this region. Supposing that this woman was invested with high authority, and wishing to have an early interview with her, we inquired of our old chief and his son where she was. They signified that she was gone far north to her winter quarters, but that she would return in about "one moon" to her southern rambles. We then made them understand that we wished to leave our vessel to live with them for a season. The three Indians consulted together for about ten minutes, when the aged sire signified their assent to our proposal, promising by signs to put food into our mouths, to give us horses to ride, to carry our luggage, and to take good care of our persons.

They wished to know how many moons we would live with them, and whether our vessel would return for us, to all of which we replied indefinitely, as all was uncertain to us.

All this took place in the cabin, the Captain and officers being present as witnesses. The chief then, by earnest gestures, inquired for our baggage, and, as it was pointed out article by article, he and his men laid hold of it, the sailors coming to their help, and in a few minutes it was all in the boat. We followed, bidding a final farewell to the Mary Jane, which had been our home for three months.

Captain Clift went on shore with us to assist in erecting our tent and to bid us a final adieu, intending to sail at evening on his voyage westward. He has taken a lively interest in all that concerns our welfare on this expedition. Our tent, which was made in New York, of light canvas, was pitched to-day for the first time. It spreads about eight feet in length and six in breadth. In this we have gathered our little all for our sojourn in Patagonia, consisting of our personal apparel, a few sheets and blankets, a small chest of medicines, a few books with stationery, two saddles with bridles and spurs, a few pounds of seabiscuit and pork, and a little bag of salt, together with a variety of articles such as axes, hatchets, files, fishing-tackle, saws, gimlets, augurs, hammers, handkerchiefs, garments, and several pieces of cotton and woollen goods, to the amount of a few hundred dollars, for presents to the savages, or to purchase food or other useful articles from them. Thus furnished, we commenced housekeeping in Patagonia on the 16th of November, 1833.

In the afternoon of this day the sealing schooner Plutarch, Captain Miner, of Mystic, Conn., came into the bay and anchored near the Mary Jane, and Captain Miner visited us in our tent on shore. At nightfall the masters, officers, and crews of the two schooners bade us a kind adieu and went on board, intending to sail that evening.

Sunday, Nov. 17. On awaking this morning

we found the Mary Jane and the Plutarch still at anchor in the harbor. A strong head-wind and a heavy current running east had prevented the vessels from leaving their anchorage. The boats of these vessels did not leave the davits all day on account of the roaring wind and the rough sea. We remained in our little tabernacle during the day; it was crowded from morning till night with the savages, all curious to examine our luggage, and even the garments on our persons. They labored hard to talk with us, and we with them; but we all found it impossible to make ourselves understood except to a very small degree.

The miserable creatures are nearly destitute of food, as this is the third day on the shore, and as they rarely find game within five to ten miles of here.

We ate sparingly of the little stores we took from the vessel, and the savages—men, women, and children—watch us like hungry dogs, and beg of us with pitiful importunity.

A few very small mussels are found along the shore, and these are the only shell-fish we have seen. Of these they gathered a scanty pittance, but not enough to satisfy hunger.

The Indians have one skin tent on the shore, and a part of them occupy this, and the rest sit and lie and sleep around upon the grass. Their time is spent in eating, when they find anything to eat, sleeping, laughing, talking, singing, card-playing, etc. Their clothing, as has been said, is of skins of the guanaco, dressed and made into mantles in the form of a blanket with the fur on. When these are old and filthy they harbor innumerable small vermin. To-day we saw one of these mantles spread out, with some six savages gathered around it. One with a club beat the fur side of the mantle, while the others watched the game as it was thrown out of the fur, seized and devoured it with greedy relish.

This is our first Sunday on heathen ground, and it is truly affecting to be surrounded by these debased and benighted beings, for whom we have so often prayed, without being able to tell them of a Saviour's love, or the motives which brought us to their dark abodes.

Nov. 18. Like yesterday and last night, this day has been boisterous on land and sea. The strong head-wind has kept the vessels at their anchors; the rain has been abundant, with chilling cold, and the clouds have been so dense and dark that, for most of the time, we have been unable to see the schooners at their anchorage. No boats have come to the shore since the 16th, and we have hardly once moved out of our quivering tent. But notwithstanding the storm, hunger has driven some of the savages to mount their horses and hunt for game. The young chief came to our tent and said in English, " Guanaco most done," and signifying that they must brave the storm and hunt. Soon a small party were mounted on horses, and armed with the *bolas*, an instrument made of strips of raw-hide about six feet long, with three strands, each armed at the end with a smooth round pebble about the size of a hen's egg, enclosed in skin. This weapon, thrown among the animals from a horse at full speed, entangles the game so that the hunter, leaping from his horse, dispatches it with his *cuchillo*, or hunting-knife.

The hunters were gone a long time, and returned at evening, weary, hungry, with dark and downcast faces, having taken nothing but one skunk.

The whole dependence of these natives for food is on their wild animals, chiefly the guanaco, which is very cautious and as fleet as the deer.

We pitied the poor fellows in their hunger and disappointment, but we had no power to help them from our slender stores, the whole of which would not have sufficed to give one tenth of them a meal.

As for fishing, though encamped on the seashore, they have no fishing-tackle, nor do they seem to know anything of the art.

But hungry and thirsty, wet and cold, without tent or fuel, they will remain on the shore as long as a vessel is at anchor. They are eager for tobacco and other stimulants, for guns and ammunition, for bread, pork, and all edibles; but tobacco and intoxicants are the first articles for which they call, and their desire for these is fearful. The articles they exchange for what they obtain from ships are fresh meat of the guanaco, furs, skin mantles, and a few other things.

The chief signified to us that they must return *mañana*, i.e. to-morrow, to their lodge in the mountains.

At 4 P.M. the storm abated and the sea was more quiet. Soon we saw the boats of the Mary Jane and the Plutarch lowered and heading for the shore. The masters, Clift and Miner, with officers and sailors, came to greet us once more and to bid us another farewell. Captain Miner brought us a basket of boiled penguins' eggs, which he had gathered at the Falkland Islands. These were very acceptable, and in our condition delicious.

At sunset the boats with our much-esteemed friends returned· to the vessels. At dark the savages, like fowls, retired to their lodgings; the horses ceased neighing, the dogs ceased howling, the children ceased their noisy gambols, the adults· ceased their hoarse talking, the wind was lulled, the sea hushed its roar; the great vault of heaven shone out adorned with glowing constellations and sprinkled with blazing sapphires. All was calm and quiet, and after offering up our vesper thanks and petitions to Him who made and who moves the mighty wheels of the universe, we fell into a sound sleep.

Nov. 19. On awaking this morning every vision of home and country, every mark of civilization, had fled. The little vessels, like sea-birds, had spread their white pinions to the breeze and sped to the west. The bark which had borne us so safely for many thousand miles, and upon which we had been so generously fed for ninety-four days, had passed away like a dream of the night.

Around us were savage horses neighing, one or two hundred savage dogs barking, and forty or fifty savage men, women, and children spread out upon the ground, some fast asleep, some snoring, some grunting, some just opening and rubbing their eyes, some jabbering, some sitting up and hunting small game in the upper loft, some smoking the nauseating pipe, some moving slowly about without apparent motive, some looking at their horses, some turning on their earthy beds "like a door on its hinges," half waking and falling asleep again. But no one was washing hands and face, no one bathing in pure water, no one reading, no one praying, no one laying a clean breakfast-table, no one cooking a morning repast, and no one eating, drinking, or even giving signs of having anything to eat! This is poverty, hunger, nakedness, filth; this is squalid misery; this is darkness and deep degradation; this is heathenism and savagism of the lowest type; this is man with the image of God erased from mind and heart—man sunk below the brute he feeds on—heaven-created man in ruins—man unconscious of his origin, utterly ignorant of what he is, of what he might be, and of all that awaits him!

Such are our surroundings, and such were some of our meditations. And how could we sound the depth or measure the length and breadth of the degradation? How, without an interpreter or any medium of communication with these deaf and dumb and blind spirits, were we to reach them?

But we are here, we thought, and these are the facts. The last material link which connected us with the civilized and Christian world is sundered. We are left among these savages without arrangement or pledge for return to our country. We are thrown upon their hospitality for our food, and upon their wills for our protection and our lives. But we do not regret it. We came voluntarily, knowing the facts, and we have no fears. "One who is faithful and true" has said, "Be not anxious for your life;" so also for "what we shall eat and drink, for your Heavenly Father knoweth that ye have need of all these things." He that "giveth to the beast his food and to the young ravens that cry" has said, "I am with you always. I will never leave or forsake you."

This was the day set for decamping and going northward, but a cold rain has prevented. So we have sat in our tent, while the Indians have filled every vacant nook and corner, watching with curious eyes every movement we make. We do all we can to communicate with them, but that is little; our thoughts are like the contents of sealed bottles ready to burst.

CHAPTER V.

VISITING THE INDIAN CAMP.

Nov. 20. Early this morning our young chief, whom we call Louis, aroused us to prepare for a march to the northward. We struck our tent at once, and prepared our luggage, which the women packed upon their horses with skill and care, having abundance of raw-hide thongs for the purpose. All the labor of pitching and of striking tents, of arranging and packing baggage, and of carrying little children, pertains to the women, while the men stand or sit and look idly on. The men carry nothing, but mount their horses like rangers, riding independently, deploying to the right and left of the trail in search of game, and rushing upon it at lightning speed when seen.

While the squaws move along in Indian file on a gentle trot, the males are seen darting off in tangents, raising the dust on many lines over the plains, or standing or wheeling on the summits of distant hills, carefully scanning the surrounding landscape in hope of descrying a herd of grazing guanacos. Whether successful or unsuccessful they soon return to the track, often ahead of the caravan, when, after moving on for a few miles in a waving line, they again repeat the old manœuvre in search of game.

The horses that we have seen thus far are small, but hardy and fleet, and quite obedient to the wills of their masters. We were surprised to see the burdens they carried. The women slung our chest (3 feet by $1\frac{1}{2}$) on one side of a horse, with a good-sized trunk on the other to balance it. On these they placed a large bag of the weight of a common travelling-trunk, and above all these a squaw mounted to guide the horse.

This is a specimen of the burdens with which they load their horses. When everything was ready, horses were assigned to Mr. Arms and myself, and as the tribe was *minus* two horses on account of their foreign guests, we were invited to take the saddle and reins and to receive a sturdy Indian each behind us. We accepted the "situation" cheerfully; for why should the dependent offer terms to his host and benefactor? So away we galloped with light hearts, for the morning was bright, the air pure, and the gratification of leaving our dingy, dreary, and hungry camp for a morning ride over the rolling prairie into the open country was exhilarating.

The moving and winding cavalcade was a picturesque one. Our faithful young chief, Louis,. led us on, and did not at first deploy like the other Indians for game. Our way led through level pampas covered with grass, and skirted at a distance on either hand with mountain ranges, some of whose summits were still shining with snow.

The travelling was good, and, though our horses were heavily laden, we proceeded at the rate of about four miles an hour. About once in ten miles the Indians would rest their horses for an hour, always near a clump of thorn-bushes when they were to be found. With these brambles they would kindle a fire and warm themselves; for though the morning was bright and the breeze gentle, yet by noon the wind became strong and cold.

We rode our own saddles and used our own bridles and spurs. The native saddle is a simple and rough imitation of the Spanish saddle-tree, made of wood and without covering. The girths and stirrup-leathers are only raw-hide straps.

The stirrup is made of wood in triangular form, and with only breadth enough to receive two toes. The spur is made of two small pieces of hard wood sharpened to a point, and rigged with leather straps so as to fasten firmly upon the heel, and tied on the instep. With these they often goad their horses until their sides run blood. The bridle-reins are raw-hide, attached to a wooden bit, which is tied to the under-jaw of the horse without headstall. With this rude bit and rein the horse is under the full control of his rider.

On our way we saw many guanacos gazing upon us from the distant hill-tops, or scudding at full-speed over the plain to avoid us. At length Louis suddenly halted, cast a keen look towards the hills on the left, and in a moment put spurs to his charger and bounded away across the plain with the speed of an arrow. This sudden movement was soon explained to us by the savages, who, pointing that way, said "Guanac! guanac!" The old chief followed his son in company with several others of the party, while we jogged on with the women, children, and luggage. In a short time young Louis rejoined our party, informed us that he had killed a guanaco, and that some of his men had remained behind to dress it. This gave us all joy, for our appetites were keen after a hungry ride of five hours. We soon came to a small bunch of bushes, where the cavalcade halted, dismounted, and kindled a fire.

Presently an Indian came up with a piece of the guanaco they had killed. This was roasted, or rather warmed and smoked, and distributed among us all.

When our scanty meal was over we proceeded on our way, the savages talking or singing in rough guttural tones. At 4 P.M. we arrived at the Indian headquarters, after a weary ride of 25 to 30 miles.

We found the savages encamped in a narrow valley between two ranges of hills which screen them from the strong winds of this country.

On our approach to this first real Indian lodge which we had seen, all the savages, old and young, men, women, and children, with a new pack of dogs, rushed out to hail us. The dogs howled, the horses neighed, the men shouted and yelled, the children screamed and ran to and fro, hiding in and behind the tents, peeping out to get a sight of the strangers and then withdrawing through fear, while the whole camp was astir with noisy interest. There were remarkable sights and sounds, and wonderful garrulity; and what odors too! In this camp we found a large number of Indians who were not on the shore. The lodge contains ten skin tents like the one on the beach. These hovels are arranged in a slightly curved line, all facing the east, as the prevailing winds are from the west. The tent in which the chief and his family live is larger and better than the rest, and is a little separated from them on the right.

A small stream of pure water runs along the valley. This is a great comfort, as water is extremely scarce in this part of the country.

There is no wood near us except a very few of the prickly bushes spoken of before, and these are used only in cooking. On our arrival the squaws unloaded the horses, delivered the baggage to its respective owners, erected the tent brought up from the bay, and assisted us in erecting ours. Meanwhile all our parcels were bestowed in a heap in the tent of the chiefs, father and son, and Louis sat by and watched them until our tent was ready, when they were brought in and arranged.

These chiefs seem to have adopted us as their children, and to feel a peculiar responsibility for our protection and comfort. All our baggage was brought safely up, even to the smallest article, and delivered to us in good condition.

Everything being thus arranged, we took possession of our little "tabernacle in the wilderness," and felt almost at home once more, though "in a strange land." Sitting in our tent door as the winds were hushed and the mild sun was sinking behind the hills, the people gathered around us, full of smiles and beckonings and wakeful curiosity; and even the little children, naked as Adam in Eden, were running and leaping and giggling in their evening gambols, often venturing near our tent, looking in upon us with curious eyes, and then with a jolly shout returning again to their plays upon the turf.

The old mother, wife of the aged chief, brought us a piece of guanaco and of pork from the Mary Jane. It was cooked in an old iron pot, and upon this we made our first meal in the inland camp of the Indians; after which we offered up our evening thanks and petitions to Him whose guardian love and care had led us thus far, and then, resting from care, enjoyed a peaceful sleep.

Nov. 21. Early in the morning the whole camp was astir, and the people flocked around our tent to watch our movements. Our hero, Louis, also came, and seeing me in the act of shaving, he begged me to take off his beard. This I did, apparently much to his gratification. Our breakfast, like our supper, was given us by the good old motherly chief, though this was evidently nearly the last morsel of meat in the tent.

Thus far we have not suffered severely from hunger, as our Indian hosts divide their scanty pittance with us. This we eat without bread or vegetables.

A party of ten, with horses, dogs, and the bolas, went out on a hunt this morning, headed by our friend, Captain Louis. Mr. Arms joined the party, while I remained to "keep ship," *i.e.* to look after the tent.

At 4 P.M. the Captain and Mr. Arms returned hungry and weary, having ridden a great distance and taken nothing. As the meat in the camp was exhausted, the savages looked gloomy and the children clamored and cried with hunger. Things were looking dark, and we began to apprehend suffering. Soon, however, another detachment of the hunting party returned with three fine guanacos slung in quarters upon their horses. Then there was laughing and shouting, and all was bright again. Before dark we were presented with a piece of meat well roasted for our supper.

The hunters also gave us an ostrich-egg measuring 14 inches in its longer and $11\frac{3}{4}$ inches in its shorter circumference. This was indeed a Godsend, as we were already longing for something besides meat for food.

I spent the day in our little tent surrounded as usual by the natives, who take great pains to communicate with us, and who seem to wonder who and what we are, whence we came, and why we have voluntarily located ourselves among them. We long to converse with them, but there is n interpreter. Probably no man on earth understands their language but themselves. They seem fond of their little children, and love to have us notice them. The children also are losing their shyness, and flock around us in a smiling and confiding way. We brought out many coarse combs, with finer ones for their use, and the little naked urchins seem delighted to have us teach them how to comb their swampy heads.

We have been examining their tents, or wigwams, and find they are made thus: Three or four rows, according to the size of the wigwam, of small stakes are set vertically in parallel lines in the ground. The first or front row may be five, six, or eight feet high, the second a foot or two shorter, and the third or fourth about two feet. On the tops of these upright stakes are slender longitudinal poles that reach from end to end of the hovel; they are lashed to the stakes with strips of skin or with the tendons of animals. This completes the frame. Over this a large covering of skins is spread and secured by thongs. The ends of the hut are secured by skins fastened to upright stakes or horizontal poles. The front is left open in fair weather; but in winter and during storms it is enclosed like the ends with curtains of skins. For this covering they use the skins of old guanacos, or those of the puma, cougar, or gray lion of South America. These skins are cut and well matched and sewed together with the sinews of animals, making blankets of convenient size, to be rolled, unrolled, spread on the tent, and removed at will. All the tents, including frames, coverings, partitions, etc., are made with reference to packing and transporting from one part of the country to another; for when a tribe or clan or division removes, nothing is left behind.

The dress of these people in its primitive state was, of course, exclusively of skins. For this purpose the skins of the calves or young guanacos were selected because of the lightness of the material, but especially on account of the softness of the fur, or rather wool. This is short, thick, and soft, like lamb's wool, interspersed with thin scattering hairs. The Indians have the art of dressing these skins with the wool on, so that they are soft and pliable like dressed deer-skin.

Thus prepared, they are cut by "dovetailing" so as to secure the greatest economy of the material, and then sewed together with a small awl of iron, which they call *hodle*, according to the size desired. The form is that of a shawl or blanket, and it is often ornamented on the flesh side with various figures colored in pigment. This is the only garment of the males, except a narrow belt of skin or cloth to cover their nakedness. It is wrapped around the person like a blanket, and in cold and stormy weather it is drawn up so as to cover the head like a hood and fastened around the waist with "a girdle of skin" like the mantle of John the Baptist. When the weather is cold the wool side is turned inward, and outward when it is warm. When hunting, the Indian girds it tight about his loins to save it from being swept off by the wind, but lets it fall from his shoulders to flutter in the wind, while the arms and upper part of the body are free for the management of the reins, the lasso, the bolas, the spear, the bow and arrow, or the knife.

The women dress like the men except that they wear a broader garment around the waist, extending from the hips to the knees. Over this the mantle is like that of the man. The foot is usually bare, but sometimes protected by moccasins made of the skin of a horse's or guanaco's leg, dressed soft and worn like a boot or stocking. They wear no head-dress but their long, coarse black hair. The small children wear "Adam-skin."

Nov. 22. Besides the young chief Louis, who has been so attentive to us, another young man claims to be a chief, under the name of Captain Lorice. He professes great friendship for us, often coming to our tent with a piece of roast meat, and trying to talk with us. When either of these chiefs is with us we have little annoyance from other visitors, but in their absence we are often troubled by the lower class of the savages, especially by mothers and children who try to examine all our baggage, often asking us with no little impudence to open all our packages and exhibit the contents. They beg relentlessly, and pilfer small articles whenever they find opportunity.

Twelve of the savages amused themselves a long time to-day by playing a game of ball. In this exercise they threw off their mantles, and exerted themselves in a state of nudity, having no clothing upon them except the strip around the loins. Their ball is nothing but a round knot of wood; their bat is a stick two feet long, and crooked at one end like the handle of a pistol. With this they drive the ball along the ground, apparently without order or system.

They have a few cards with which they occasionally play, but we have seen no gambling as yet.

At noon Captain Louis led up a horse in front of his cabin, when another Indian, standing about six feet in front of the animal, shot an arrow into his breast. The arrow penetrated eighteen inches, entering the heart. In a few minutes the horse staggered and fell dead, and soon it was dressed and prepared for cooking—head, feet, entrails, and all. Shortly after several pieces were brought to us roasted. On these we dined. The horse was fat, and the meat tender and not unpalatable, especially for men in our hungry condition.

As the savages find their game so wild and fleet that it cannot be procured without vigorous exertions, and as they are supremely indolent, they are quite liable to get out of food, when their only recourse is to slaughter a horse. Though they caught three guanacos yesterday, all were consumed at once; for, divided among a hundred half-starved people, there was but a small pittance for each individual.

This afternoon we found that a good cord belonging to our tent was missing. Of this we informed Louis, who immediately commenced a search from hovel to hovel, until he found and restored it to us. He seemed to feel badly on account of the affair, and many of the savages gathered around us to protest their own innocence of the offence. This showed some sense of right and wrong in their minds, and our action in the case seemed to impress them favorably. At first we debated the question as to the prudence, in this early stage of our acquaintance with the Indians, of complaining of this petty theft; but as it was obvious that even these ignorant beings had some notions of the right, and as we feared that a neglect to notice the affair would embolden them to further depredations, we resolved to be decided with them in the outset, and, if possible, to check the evil in the bud. Thus far the effect is decidedly favorable. The chiefs tell us that they must soon remove to some place where guanacos are plenty, and ask if we will go with them. Of course we have no alternative, as our lives depend on their supply of food. Our lot is cast with the savages for better or for worse, and we wish to travel wherever they go, to see the country.

Nov. 23. The weather has been fine for most of the time since we came up into the country. Gentle spring showers are frequent, and the air is mild and salubrious.

Early in the morning I rambled out and climbed one of the highest peaks of the northern range of hills under which we are encamped. It is covered with grass to its summit, and I saw three guanacos feeding on its side. I also started a gray fox, an animal common in this country.

From the top of this hill I had a grand and extended view of the surrounding country. The landscape consists of vast plains, studded here and there with isolated conical hills, and skirted by low mountain ranges. But silence and desolation reign everywhere. No voice of man or beast or bird echoed through the stillness. The three guanacos shot off at reindeer speed, and were soon out of sight, and the fox sneaked noiselessly away and disappeared. No pretty villages nestled among shade-trees; no lowing herds, or bleating flocks, or gamboling lambkins gave life and beauty to the landscape, or broke its everlasting slumbers.

I returned to the camp, and found it almost desolate. A large company of Indians had gone out on a hunting expedition, while most of the available women and children went a long distance to the hills, where they gathered fungus excrescences from old trees. These fungi consist of small globular masses, quite dry and tasteless, which the savages eat with their meat as we would eat popped corn. They returned at evening with small quantities of this insipid article, which they call *chouet* and of which they seem fond. They gave us a little, and we eat it for want of bread or vegetables.

Our camp has been quiet, as so many have been absent and we have not experienced our usual annoyances.

We have been well supplied with horse-beef to-day, roasted or boiled in an old iron pot, and brought to us by the savages when they took their own meals.

The hunting party returned with seven guanacos, and our food is just now abundant. Captain Louis brought me a pair of trousers to-day, received on board the Mary Jane, and requested me to piece them, as they are too small! He often brings us little tasks, and seems much pleased by our ability and readiness to help him. He has spent much of the day with us, and he exhibits the same inquiring disposition, often asking us the names of things in English, and then giving us their Patagonian names. We are more and more pleased with his kindness, and feel glad to have him with us. He loves to imitate Americans, and occasionally comes out in a full sailor's dress which he has obtained of some passing vessel.

The old chief, father of Louis, had a severe colic to-day, and groaned heavily with pain. Mr. Arms gave him a sedative, which soon relieved the pain and surprised the gazing savages.

Our almost constant music during the day is the noise of children and the barking and yelling of dogs. These animals are extremely poor, and whenever meat or bones are thrown out to them there is a horrid squabble of a whole pack, and the weaker escape limping from the jaws of the stronger with yells which are piercing. Besides this their owners are almost constantly beating them with clubs, keeping up an incessant uproar in the canine family.

Sunday, Nov. 24. The Indians had a long game at ball-play this forenoon; otherwise the day has been quiet. We have never seen our young chief Louis at a game of ball. Is it because he regards his dignity too highly? We cannot say. As yet we have seen nothing which looks like religious rites among this people, nor do we know whether they have any notions of a Supreme Being or a future state of existence. They have crude ideas of right and wrong. They praise and blame. The thief is shy and shows a sense of fear and guilt; and the man who has lost a knife, a file, or a piece of meat by a thief is full of rage and cursing. Of course their moral code, or their distinction between right and wrong, is very imperfect. We are forcibly impressed, however, with the truth asserted by Paul in regard to the heathen who have not the Scriptures: "These having not the law, are a law unto themselves; who show the work of the law written in their hearts, their conscience also bearing witness, and their thoughts the mean while accusing or else excusing one another."

Most of this day we have spent in our little tabernacle, where we have been visited by many of the Indians, who have been very civil; and we have tried to interest them by signs. But ah! it is hard to be surrounded by these gazing, chattering savages without being able to teach them of "the true God and Eternal Life." We long for an interpreter, to open an avenue to their understandings and hearts. But our desires are vain.

These savages seem to look upon us as of a superior race of beings, and they are more and more careful not to do things which appear to displease us, often quietly *asking* liberty to come into our tent, and carefully avoiding meddling with our furniture without leave.

We show them maps and pictures, and interest them with object-lessons so far as we have the means to teach them. The effect of checking them when noisy and rude, and in every effort to commit petty depredations, appears favorable; and thus we are enabled to impress them with some moral lessons and to lead them in some degree. We look upon them with pity and compassion, and they gaze upon us with unceasing wonder.

Nov. 25. Cold and uncomfortable. Spent most of the day in our tent making a flannel shirt for our chief. He watches the work with great interest, and many others crowd around to see us use the needle. All our operations are watched by scores of curious eyes.

A grand hunt to-day, and the party returned at evening with ten guanacos. Captain Louis brought home a fine young calf, and presented it whole and undressed to us. This gives us a good supply for several days; but we have no salt for preserving meat. The natives use no salt, although there is salt in the interior; but the air is cold and pure, and meat can be kept three days by hanging it out in the wind. When their fresh meat is abundant they jerk it, then smoke and pound it into a Patagonian pemmican. This they often preserve against a famine, a long storm, or winter when the snows are deep. Hitherto we have let the Indians bring us our food cooked. To-morrow we propose to commence cooking for ourselves, as their cookery is wretched.

Nov. 26. After retiring last evening, we heard for a long time what appeared to be a speech or harangue in the tent of our chief. The tones of voice expressed great earnestness and anima-

VISITING THE INDIAN CAMP. 85

tion, and were finely modulated for a public speaker.

What the nature and occasion of this declamation were we are unable to learn. Our ears were also saluted by harsh, monotonous singing in some of the tents for most of the night, so that we slept but little.

To-day, by permission of our hosts, we commenced cooking our own food. And though our bill of fare is still limited to one article, we find a decided improvement in our meals.

During our culinary operations the natives crowded around in large numbers, and with an intense curiosity, wondering at our strange manœuvres. We can practise but three modes of cooking—roasting, frying, and boiling—but these will give us a little variety in our dishes.

Nov. 27. This day has passed like most of the days since we came to this camp. The poor savages lounge around us from morning to night, unless hunger drives them out to hunt. They both excite our sympathy and try our patience. Most of them are quiet and civil when they pay us a visit, but one woman is more troublesome than all the rest of the tribe ; indeed we both agree that she is the most vexatious creature we ever met in human form. She is large, ill-formed, dark-visaged, greasy, and filthy. These physical defects we could endure; but her spiritual composition seems to consist of all that is revolting in impudence and villainy. Her visits are long and frequent; she seems determined to handle and examine every bag, box, trunk, and all other articles in our tent; and she is perpetually begging for herself and children, of whom she has a large brood. She rarely fails to be present at our meals, looking into our saucepan, peeping into every dish, and begging everything we cook. To-day she had the assurance to dash her brawny hand into our soup and haul out some of the meat. This was not occasioned by hunger, as there is now an abundance of meat in her tent. We treat her with as much inattention as possible, and have resolved to give her nothing she asks for until she ceases her impudent begging, persuaded that to gratify her wishes would only make her visits more frequent and her demands more intolerable.

Sometimes she seems vexed by our neglect, and leaves us in a pet, growling and muttering as she goes; and we indulge the momentary hope that we shall have less of her company henceforth. But she soon returns to the attack with renewed vigor, and we have only to entrench ourselves again with apparent indifference, and thus to stand on the defensive until the storm is over. Such cases only impress us more and more with the absolute degradation of these savages.

Nov. 28. Cold and dreary. We spend a large portion of our time in reading, writing, and studying Spanish.

We hear that there are some Indians in other clans who know more Spanish and English words than any we have yet met. We learn, also, that there are several runaway captive sailors among the northern clans, and that these clans will soon visit us, with the queen, Maria, and these English and American captives. We therefore await with great interest their arrival, hoping to find some better medium of communication than we now have, and thus to learn more of the country and its inhabitants.

The Indians come to us in crowds, filling our tent, squatting before the door, and straining their black eyes to look in and see what we are doing. Many of them are pleasant in their demeanor, and bring us pieces of meat. But we depend chiefly upon our host, Louis, to supply our wants.

Our mode of cooking and eating affords them

Missing Page

Missing Page

CHAPTER VI.

A SQUALL.

Nov. 30. We wrote nothing yesterday.

What we feared on the 28th came upon us on the 29th. Early yesterday morning Lorice and his Jezebel came to see us, and wished us to strike our tent and prepare to go with them—where, we of course did not know. Many of the women were taking down their hovels and preparing all their stuff for removing, while the men were bringing up their horses for decamping. We looked at the tent of Louis, which was still untouched. But as most of the tents around were coming down we felt it prudent to begin arranging our luggage, lest we should be left alone. Meanwhile the chief, Lorice, with his Jezebel were assailing Louis and his friends with angry language. She especially seemed full of fury, and her face and eyes looked fiendish, and we every moment looked for blows. At length, however, there was a calm, and we hoped that the squall was over. We struck our tent, and Louis struck his. Jezebel came and took a small medicine-chest and some other articles, and packed them on her horse. Other squaws took other articles, until one half or more of our baggage was upon horses.

All at once the storm broke upon us with double fury. Jezebel dashed our chest of medicines on the ground, breaking vials and doing much damage; then she threw off all our luggage and scattered it hither and thither, storming and raging like a fury. At once the clan began to resolve itself into two hostile parties; the larger number clinging to Lorice and his vixen, and the smaller ranging with our friend Louis. The war of words went on and waxed hotter and hotter, till it assumed the fury of a whirlwind. At length the vixen with her whelps flew at the hair and eyes of our friend, and he was thrown upon the ground, kicked, scratched, beaten, his hair pulled out, his ear-jewels rent from his ears; he was soon smeared with sweat, dirt, and blood. Louis's party came to his help, but the opposite side outnumbered them two to one, and the weaker party were roughly handled. Many were thrown upon the ground and dragged by the hair, with faces and limbs begrimed with dust and blood. The old chiefs, Louis's father and mother, tall, venerable savages of not less than seventy years, fought desperately for their son and his family. But they, too, were overpowered by numbers and thrown upon the ground.

It was a miserable sight, while the struggle was going on, to see the bloody and beseeching face of Louis, as he lay prostrate on the ground, grasping with one hand a large bag of clothing and various articles belonging to us, and with the other trying to protect himself from his savage foes, and beckoning to us to come and help him in protecting our own property. But we had, alas! no power to help. We sat on the ground in full view of the trying scene, and could only signify by looks and gestures our disapproval, and our wish to see peace and harmony restored.

At length the struggle abated from the sheer exhaustion of the combatants, and the parties, with torn ears, noses, and skins, and with dishevelled hair, sat down in two lines, facing each other in sullen silence. We improved the armistice in endeavoring by signs and looks to make a peace. But hot blood was up, and the flinty Patagonian wills were not yet softened. After a short breathing-spell the two lines rose and attacked each other again in a hand-to-hand fight as before; while we again looked on with amazement and grief, not knowing how the strife would end.

But the second struggle was shorter than the first, and again the parties sat down exhausted. An Indian who had always appeared mild and friendly then rose, and commenced to harangue both parties in eloquent tones. He spoke for about fifteen minutes, and in such a manner as to chain the attention of all. His speech was marked with energy, animation, and pathos; he had varied and melodious intonations of voice, and used seemingly appropriate gestures. Of course we regretted exceedingly that we could not understand his language.

All was hushed during the harangue; and in a few minutes after its close, the parties rose up, brought together their strayed horses, gathered the scattered *débris* of the fight, and reloaded the animals, each party furnishing half the horses for the luggage. One party brought a horse to Mr. Arms, and the other party one for me. This amicable settlement by compromise revealed the cause of the fight. Each party wanted to keep the strangers, and neither would yield its claims until exhausted by fighting. This reminded us of what men call civilized and Christianized warfare. Had these savages reasoned better, they would have settled their respective claims by arbitration or by mutual concessions and agreement without a fight. But in savage and in civilized warfare, after blood has been shed, property destroyed, misery inflicted, and hatred engendered, the parties come back upon the right ground of settlement, that of negotiation and reason.

It was fortunate for these Patagonians that they were not armed with deadly weapons. We saw no fire-arms, bows and arrows, knives, or clubs in use on this occasion; and no lives were sacrificed.

At $3\frac{1}{2}$ P.M. we were again ready for our march, and after travelling some ten miles over a northern ridge, we encamped at $6\frac{1}{2}$ in a quiet notch in the mountains. Here we erected our tent, kindled a fire, and prepared our supper. Our friend Louis came to our help, and brought us the head and neck of a guanaco which he had killed by the way.

Thus after a day of fatigue and solicitude we were permitted to lie down once more in peace.

During the live-long night the Indians were

very noisy, singing, talking, and haranguing. This interrupted our sleep, yet we had no fears, as all seemed good-natured, with no evidence of anger or contention.

Perhaps they were like soldiers in camp, rehearsing the dangers escaped, the skill and cunning of the tactics, the valor and prowess displayed, the trophies won, and the glories which crowned the field and the fight.

Early this morning a large party took up their horses and went off on a grand hunt, and we have been permitted to spend a quiet and peaceful day in writing and study.

Sunday, Dec. 1. The place of our new encampment is somewhat similar to the one we left. We are in a cosey nook among hills, with grassy valleys in the near vicinity, and surrounded with prairie-lands studded with conical, truncated, and elongated sand-dunes. On the pampas the grass is coarse and bunchy. In the alluvial valleys the soil is rich and the grasses luxuriant. Everywhere the soil is sandy, and, what strikes us as remarkable, we have not yet seen a rock, a boulder, or a pebble big enough to throw at a bird.

A rill of pure water runs along our valley, and,

as is usual, a little clump of thorny bushes is near by.

These shrubs are now in leaf and blossom, and from extreme longing for cereals or vegetable food I go to these bushes to browse, eating the leaves, buds, and flowers. They are slightly acid, and afford a little relief to the strong appetite for some other food than flesh.

Not succeeding yesterday, the savages have gone out to-day on another hunt. This is the first Sabbath they have chanced to spend thus since we have been among them.

This morning "Jezebel" came to visit us again. We had indulged the hope that after the fight of the memorable 29th her visits would be "few and far between," and brief withal. But all disputes being amicably settled between the belligerents, on she comes again. With face lighted up like moonshine upon a thunder-cloud, she invited me to go to her husband's tent and receive a piece of meat. I went and brought the present; but it was only a few minutes before she returned and began begging this thing and that, with her characteristic audacity. It was a long time before we could get rid of her, and when she turned her broad back we breathed freely again.

This is the first visit we have received from any of the Lorice family since the fight. The reason evidently is because they cannot succeed in detaching us from our old and tried friends the Louis family.

The savages, as before stated, pitch their tents nearly in a straight line, the old chief and his son on the right and Lorice on the left. Our tent is again pitched close to Louis's.

My companion has been ailing to-day, so that he has kept his bed. Probably this is, in part at least, on account of the great change in our diet and the fatigue and excitement of the two days past.

The wife of the old chief has come to our tent several times to-day to look after the sick man. She appears very sympathetic, and evidently longs to do something to help him. We are becoming not a little attached to this fine old woman, and begin to call her mother. Her husband is a patriarchial man in appearance. Each of them is six feet high, and they are venerable in their three score and ten years. There is something so noble, so kind, and so generous in this aged couple that we are strongly drawn toward them. How ardently we long to bring the invitations of the

Gospel to them! for we almost feel assured that while thousands of the youth and the well-informed in our land reject the "glad tidings," this aged couple would receive the truth with the docility of little children.

Dec. 2. Mr. Arms is well again. We washed some clothes to-day, and the Indians gathered around us in droves. All appeared full of curiosity on seeing the process. Probably they had never seen washing before, for although there are a few cotton and woollen garments, such as shirts, among them, yet we have never seen them wash *anything*, not even their hands and faces, nor have we ever seen one of them bathe, or a mother wash her pappoose.

The old chief and his wife made us a long, friendly visit to-day. They seem very cordial and paternal in their friendship, and we enjoyed their visit.

During their stay our thorny "Jezebel" came and looked in at our door, but seeing us entertaining some of the family she hates, she turned herself and went off with an air of bitter contempt. We were glad thus to escape another siege, and felt under much obligation to our aged friends for protecting our castle from an attack.

A SQUALL. 99

At evening we closed our tent early and observed the monthly concert of prayer. This is the first season of. the kind we have spent on heathen ground. We were but "two" in number, yet we had the promise of a third, and this was a joy. We had often prayed for the heathen before, but never before among the heathen. We had often prayed for missionaries before, but never before with such a knowledge of the trials and the wants of missionaries.

Dec. 3. It is midsummer with us, and while our northern homes are ice-bound we are bathing in a hot summer sun. Our Indians are now well supplied with food, and, in accordance with their lazy habits, some are snoozing in their cabins and others are stretched out upon the ground, basking like seals in the solar rays. There will be no more hunting and no more labor until their present supply of meat shall be exhausted.

Thus far our fears of suffering from hunger have not been realized. He that "heareth the young ravens when they cry" has liberally spread our table, if not with the luxuries, yet with the necessaries of life.

Dec. 4. Rambling this morning in search of edible roots or greens, many children followed me, and perceiving me digging the ground, as if hunting for something, they pointed out a small bulb which, as they signified, was edible. We dug a small mess and boiled them, finding them quite refreshing, though we had never seen the savages eat them. Their appearance is like that of a small garlic, and the taste somewhat like a turnip. They were, however, very scarce, and we never found them in any other place.

A little before noon we perceived a movement in the camp, and in a few minutes every tent except that of the old chief and family was struck and the houses packed for decamping. This sudden and to us mysterious movement was ordered by the chief Lorice; but for what reason we could not determine. Previously, when the Indians were about to remove, they have given us timely notice and invited us to go with them. On this occasion nothing was said to us until most of the clan had moved off.

As our host Louis remained quiet all this time, we went to inquire what this meant. He signified that the party in motion were going out to meet the old queen Maria, and that he and his small family would remain and look after us until their return. Meanwhile Lorice lingered about the camp-ground until all of his party had left. He then made us a call of some twenty minutes, and departed to follow his party. Louis rode out with them some distance, but returned before night bringing a fresh guanaco which he had killed on the way, and of which he gave us nearly half.

We are now left with a single family, formerly consisting of the old chief and wife and five children: two sons and three daughters. The two older sisters and a woman whom we supposed to be Louis's wife went off with the clan, leaving only the old couple and Louis with a brother and sister younger than he, five in all, with us. Where we shall go next, or what the morrow will reveal, is all uncertain. All is quiet, and in the deserted camp there is a feeling of solitude which is a little oppressive.

Dec. 5. The peace and stillness around make it seem like a Sabbath. No romping and squalling children, no rude and noisy men, and few dogs are to be heard.

Seeing a dozen guanacos on a distant hill, our chief offered me his gun and wished me to go in pursuit of them. Accordingly I went, and after walking about two miles I came in full view of more than thirty feeding in a herd. At a distance they resembled a drove of colts; on being approached they neighed like colts. "I came, I saw;" the animals, too, saw—and snorted and disappeared. I returned with gun and charge, heated and wearied, but with no game. It is next to impossible to get near enough to a guanaco to bring him down with a rifle.

Dec. 6. Having intimated to our host that we needed more covering at night, he immediately presented us with several young guanaco-skins, and his mother and sister set about making them into a bed-spread for us.

We have only to make known our wants to this family and they are at once supplied to the extent of their ability. Our Indian mother still treats us with true kindness, and endeavors to prevent all unnecessary annoyances. If the dogs become troublesome while we are dressing our meat, or cooking, she comes with her rod to chastise them and to teach them manners. The two children appear affectionate and obedient. They never trouble us like many of the other children when they visit us, and they show no inclination to pilfer little articles. In point of intellect, sprightliness, and pleasantry they would not suffer by comparison with many children of civilized countries.

Dec. 7. Louis went out on a hunt and brought in a large supply of fresh meat, which he shared liberally with us. When we are overstocked with venison, we jerk a part and keep it against a time of scarcity.

Our chief tells us that he belongs to a large tribe who have spent the winter far north, where the climate is mild, and that they are now coming south by easy marches and will soon be here. So he remains to receive them. He also says that Lorice and his clan are aliens from Tierra del Fuego, and that the northern Patagonians do not associate with them; also that they go by themselves most of the time. He says that the reason why he associated with them is because he took a woman of that clan, and that she had now left him and gone off with her friends.

We are picking up Patagonian words daily, and our chief is very eager to get hold of English words.

These quiet days afford us an excellent time for reading, writing, study, and conversation with our neighbors, who appear more and more attached to us.

We are very anxious to see more of the country, to meet other tribes, and, if possible, to obtain horses and guides to take us over the western mountains to the Pacific coast, somewhere in the region of Chiloe or among the Araucanians south of Chili. As it now is, however, we are shut up to faith and hope, and we must wait the will of our Master, and move only when the cloud-pillar lifts and goes forward. We are in an unknown wilderness, surely, where all is wild and strange, utterly helpless in ourselves even to secure our daily food. We can pray as never before: "Guide us, O thou great Jehovah," adding with special earnestness, "give us day by day our daily bread!"

The day has been cold, with frequent falls of rain and hail. Mr. Arms is still feeble.

Dec. 8. Our host has been out and brought in a guanaco. A heavy frost covered the ground this morning, and the day has been cold and squally. Angry clouds have been passing over, and frequently discharging their chilling contents of rain and hail. We wrap ourselves up in skins and keep quiet in our quivering tent.

Dec. 9. This morning our young chief went out again with bolas, knife, and dogs on a hunt for guanacos. His aged father, who has been mostly kept to the camp for a long time by inflamed eyes and the infirmities of old age, also saddled his steed and followed his son to the chase. The day proved uncomfortable for the expedition, the wind being quite piercing and the rain falling almost continuously. Notwithstanding this the Indians returned with eleven guanacos, most of which were young ones, as these sooner tire under the chase and are easily caught by the dogs. Of these calves they gave us three as our portion.

Thus the Lord spreads our table by the hands of these savages, whose hearts he has moved to receive and support us with a kindness and hospitality truly affecting.

Dec. 10. Prepared a little spot of ground and planted some garden-seeds to-day, though we shall probably soon remove to some other place, and may never see this spot again. We have also planted the seeds of various kinds of fruit-trees, which we hope may yet spring up and bear fruit, though we do not see it. The restless, roaming habits of these natives render it impossible to attend to agriculture among them. Captain Louis went out and returned with a horse-load of long poles and stakes to hang fresh meat upon. The wood resembles wild cherry. He must have brought them from a great distance, as he was gone nearly all day. Two of his largest stakes he gave to us for our use.

Dec. 13. On the 11th and 12th nothing occurred worthy of record. To-day our friend signified that we must soon break up camp and go eastward. Asking him why, he only replied that this place is " malo."

We could not understand this complaint, as our wants have never been so well provided for as since we came to this station. The reason of this evidently is that we are few in numbers and very quiet; therefore the game is not frightened away by the noise of dogs, the yells of savages, and the rush of the chase. And again it is the season of calving, when it is easy for one or two Indians, with twenty to thirty dogs, to run down the young and weak animals. But to make swoop upon a herd of keen-eyed and watchful full-grown guanacos is quite another thing, and to secure large numbers of them often requires combination and strategy such as the Patagonian hunter only understands. Sometimes they go out fifty or a hundred strong, on a grand hunt, with from one to three hundred dogs, the dogs and horses being thoroughly trained to the service. In such cases one or two scouts are sent quietly out to examine the meadows and valleys where the animals feed. When a herd is descried the utmost caution is observed, so as not to discover an Indian to the herd. The hunters then deploy to the right and left, keeping under cover of hills, or in ravines, if possible, until they have formed a circle around the herd, the dogs keeping close to their masters. They then quietly contract the circle until the guanacos take the alarm, when the whole herd, following one leader, rushes for some point in the circle to break it and escape. At this moment dogs and horses all start for that point, and those which reach it before the guanacos seize the game. A score or two of bolases are whirled in the air and sent whizzing among the animals, winding around their necks and entangling their legs, while the dogs fall upon the prey, and the Indians, leaping from their horses and cutting the throats of the game with their sheath-knives, drink the hot blood with their dogs.

They then sever the trunk of the animal midway between the fore and hind legs, and lashing one half on one side and the other on the opposite side of the saddle, they mount again and fly over the plains shouting like triumphant conquerors returning from a gory field.

Dec. 14. We have been one month in Patagonia to-day. This morning Louis came and said to us, " Much Indus in Gregory's Bay," and then signified that to-morrow there would be a *pigo grande* (a great smoke), and that we all should move down to the Strait. He intimated that Lorice and his party had gone thither by a circuitous route which he described on the ground; and that Queen Maria had come with her train. He also gave us to understand that to-morrow she would send for us to go down to her camp.

Anxious to know whether we understood our chief, it was proposed that one of us go down with him to the Strait and see what was the state of the case. To this he assented, and in a few minutes two horses were ready and I set off at rapid speed with the young man, while Mr. Arms remained "by the stuff."

Our track to the sea was a new one to me; it led over lofty hills, across broad plains, and through deep winding ravines.

On our way we saw hundreds of guanacos feeding in the meadows, several droves of which we pursued for a considerable distance; but though our horses skimmed the ground like arrows, yet horses and dogs were distanced by the elastic bounds of these swift creatures, which were soon out of sight.

These horses are so thoroughly trained for the chase that as soon as the scent of the game is snuffed, or the neighing heard, they are restless as the war-horse at the booming of cannon or the smell of gunpowder, and the instant the signal is given they dart for the prey, bounding over meadows and plains, over morasses, bogs, and ravines, rising and descending very steep hills with little abatement of speed, and suffering nothing to obstruct their progress till they are checked by their riders or fall breathless with fatigue. In going directly over a steep hill of about 700 feet elevation, and on an angle of 35° to 40°, our horses climbed with amazing energy, and on descending on the opposite side they threw themselves on their haunches, leaping rapidly with their fore-feet, and suffering their hinder parts to slide after them. This was a new way of "coasting," but it worked well with the rider as he sat firmly in his saddle. While I enjoyed the motion, I admired the skill of the animals.

Divest European cavalry of fire-arms, and allow them only the sabre and lance, and they would stand a poor chance before the Patagonian cohorts armed with the bolas and knife.

We caught no guanacos, and having taken no *viaticum* we began to feel hungry. Fortunately, however, the keen hunter's eye of Louis descried a little *cochin*, or skunk, in a bunch of grass. Dismounting quietly, he thrust his hand into the grass and hauled out pussy so adroitly as to kill it without the least accident to himself. He then hung it upon his saddle, mounted his steed, and on we rushed. Coming in full view of Gregory's Bay, and gaining an extended sight of the Strait and shores, we saw no smoke, no wigwams, and no Indians.

It was now late in the afternoon; we had ridden some thirty miles; the wind had become strong and cold. We turned our horses' heads northward and rode against a wind which soon became so violent that it was difficult to keep in our saddles, and our horses put down their heads, snorted, and almost refused to move. Louis dismounted, ordered me to dismount, and said that we must spend the night where we were. We unsaddled our horses, and Louis, tying their fore-feet together so that they could make progress only by leaping, let them go for the night. His next movement was to cook his game for supper. At a short distance he found a small clump of bushes, where he kindled a fire, in the flame of which he singed off the hair of the skunk. Then, having heated some small stones which he carried with him, he put them into the bowels of the *cochin*, and laying it among the embers and smoke of his improvized oven, it was soon roasted to his satisfaction. Tearing off one quarter he gave it to me, and appropriating the other three quarters, with the appurtenances, he devoured it all in less time than has been occupied in this description. Nothing was left of his portion, for even the bones were cracked and the marrow sucked out.

Night coming on, we now prepared to sleep. Placing our saddles at our heads and near the bushes, as a small barrier against the wind, and taking our saddle-cloths for blankets, we lay down while the blasts raved and roared around us. In the night we were aroused by one of the horses, who in his struggle to free himself of his unwelcome fetters came leaping and stumbling within a few feet of us, greatly endangering our safety. Louis arose, unshackled both the horses, and tied them to tufts of grass; and we were undisturbed till morning.

Sunday, Dec. 15. We arose early to return to our camp, but our horses were not to be found. They had broken from their tetherings and made their escape. We were a little perplexed, but the morning was calm and bright. Directing me to remain and keep still in my place, Louis set off in search of the stray beasts. Thus I was left alone in this vast wilderness without power to find my way back to the camp, as I had left my pocket-compass behind and had taken no bearings, trusting alone to my guide and expecting to return with him on Saturday to the lodge. But if I had not taken my compass, I had not forgotten my little pocket Testament, my constant companion in sleeping and waking. Nor could I forget the assuring promise in Heb. xiii. 5: "For he hath said, I will never leave thee nor forsake thee." So I sat on the ground and mused; I arose and walked to and fro; I looked north, south, east, and west, but no sound was heard and no moving thing was seen. "Both the beast and the bird were fled, they were gone." I took out my watch and looked; one half-hour gone and no Louis. Again I looked; one hour gone and he had not returned. The third half-hour went, and I stood alone in a vast and unknown solitude—in a realm of utter silence, and silence that, like the darkness of Egypt, "could be felt." Never before had I so impressively realized the value of a man, savage though that man be. How truthfully came the words of Isaiah to mind, "I will make a man more precious than fine gold"!

Looking and waiting, I wandered to a small bunch of bushes, and here I found a hawk's nest, with one young half-fledged hawk. Hunger was on me, and now, thought I, we shall have a breakfast when our chief returns with the horses. I worked my way into the brambles and caught the bird. He fought bravely for "life and liberty" and with beak and talons drew blood, but hunger conquered and I secured him. Shortly after this capture, back came my hero with both of the truants. At this my heart leaped for joy, the waiting had seemed so long and painful; but when he saw the bird in my keeping his face grew dark as a thunder-cloud, and he seemed to be in rage and consternation. He began to gesticulate earnestly and to cry out, "Malo! malo!" shaking his head significantly, till I was alarmed, and ran back to the bush with my prey and restored the bird to its nest. Thus all my fond hopes of a breakfast were dashed. I suppose that this hawk is sacred to the Patagonians, and that their superstitious fears forbid to do it harm. Our horses were saddled and mounted in haste, and after a John Gilpin ride of five hours we reached our camp about noon, weary and hungry, as I had gone thirty-six hours with no other food than a small piece of *cochin*.

My "companion in arms" had been anxious for us, and he had thoughtfully boiled a piece of guanaco for me. In a little tent as we are, and in a wild and savage land, the sight of our tabernacle was truly cheering, because it has the name, and has by use something of the air, of home. We trust we are truly thankful for our shelter, and that our circumstances are so much better than they might be. On our way back this morning young Louis pointed out a place to which he said we would soon remove.

Dec. 16. Found the Indians preparing for a removal this morning; but as it was rainy and cold we advised them to wait until to-morrow, to which they cheerfully assented. So we spend the day in preparing our baggage for decamping.

Dec. 17. Agreeably to the arrangements of yesterday we struck our tent early this morning, put our effects on horses provided for us, and set out with our Indian family for the new place of encampment. Our course was eastward, and our removal occupied most of the day. The new location is near a small stream of water, but it is in an open plain of wide extent, surrounded in the distance by hills which bound our horizon. Here we have nothing but a few bushes, near which we have pitched our tent, to break the force of the winds as they come sweeping over the pampas.

Before we had time to erect our tent a cold rain came on that wet both our luggage and ourselves and rendered us very uncomfortable. The chief's family, with their usual kindness, rendered us every assistance in their power, though this help came mostly from the women.

Dec. 18. A cold and blustering day. The wind rushes, screeches, and howls. Our tent quivers and shakes and threatens to fall. It already begins to give way before the blasts, and we have been obliged to take it down to mend the threatening rents. It is quite too frail to last long in this climate, and unless we can keep screened from the winds among the hills or in quiet valleys, our tabernacle will soon take wings and leave us. It could not possibly stand during a winter. Should it fail us we must take lodgings in the skin hovels of the Indians. This will be uncomfortable indeed, as their tents are made loathsome by grease, old skins, filth, vermin, the smoke of their cooking, and the almost unendurable smoke of their pipes. Add to this their numerous lousy, gaunt, and quarrelling dogs, twenty or thirty of them to each hut, and one can imagine the situation without a desire to test it by sight, or sound, or smell, or touch.

It is difficult to conceive of a lower state of existence than we find in Patagonia.

Dec. 19. This morning Mr. Arms went out with Louis and his young brother to seek a fresh supply of meat, while our kind Indian mother with her little daughter returned to the place of our last sojourn to bring some stakes and poles which we had left behind because our horses were overloaded on the 17th, but which we needed.

Thus I am left with no one in the lodge but the old chief, who is still much indisposed and almost blind with inflamed eyes. The quiet is impressive, and the relief for a few hours from the discordant sounds of an Indian camp is very grateful.

While thus congratulating myself on the uninterrupted solitude in prospect, all at once two Indians on foot arrived with tidings that our old acquaintance Captain Lorice with his unctuous wife Jezebel and the large party that separated from us two weeks ago were on their way back and would soon be here. Soon after several other Indians came up, and presently the whole troop of horses appeared. The riders dismounted, and the squaws at once set about pitching their tents in a line, with ours on the right, while the men and children gathered around me, the women joining them as soon as the tents were erected. All appeared good-natured and joyful at meeting, as if old feuds and jealousies were forgotten. From this time till night our tent was thronged with these children of nature, filling every nook within and crowding around the door in almost stifling numbers, all apparently curious to know if any change had come over the " Americana" strangers during their absence.

One of the Indians brought me a fine saddle of young guanaco, another filled my hands with jerked meat pulverized, and Captain Lorice presented me with a whole calf and made a long and friendly visit. As soon as his wife had erected and arranged her tent she also came with seeming great good-nature, smiling as if she had been transformed into "an angel of light," and bringing with her the old brood of children. It was not long, however, before this April sunbeam was obscured by peevish and fitful clouds. "The ruling passion," cupidity, still strong, began to show itself. With her usual disgusting impudence she set to handling our effects, asking me to open bags and cases and show her all our goods, at the same time reminding me of the present her husband had just given me, in order to impress me with a due sense of obligation. But she found me imperturbable and unpersuasible, and after vainly trying every art in her power, in tones and looks and earnest gesticulations, pointing to her rags, hauling up her children to show their nudity, and even opening their mouths to signify their desire to eat our food, she became sullen and silent.

At evening our little party returned with thirty young calves, having had unparalleled success. Of these twelve were given to us. This appears to be the season of plenty with the Indians.

Dec. 20. Visited to-day by large numbers of the natives. They appear so fond of our society and so curious to see us at our work that they almost crowd us out of our tent. While dressing our game they flocked around and begged the liver, lungs, kidneys, heart, etc. These they devoured raw with the greediness of carnivorous animals. This is not occasioned by hunger, as they are now well fed; but it is a habit of theirs, and they esteem these parts (especially when they come warm from the animal) as a great luxury. I have seen the children eating the most offensive parts of the intestines uncooked and unwashed; and the blood is a sweet beverage to all.

The Indians find wild dandelions in this region, and they gather and eat them in large quantities, roots, stems, and all, without washing or boiling. Thus it seems we are not alone in our keen desire for vegetables and herbs.

Toward evening Captain Lorice made us a long visit, and again urgently requested us to leave the family by whose kind care we have been so long fed and go with him and his tribe to the north. He offers to give us each a fine horse, to feed us well, and to protect and guide us wherever he travels. He continues to show his envy of Louis, and calls him and his family by ill names, while he boasts of his own greatness and goodness.

If one would believe it, he is a model of all righteousness, truth, and generosity. His invitation was pressed with much earnestness by some of his favorites, who labored to impress us with a sense of his excellences, assuring us we should lack nothing if we would put ourselves under his care.

But we are still deaf to the entreaties and incredulous to the fair promises of this chief and his clan, and we feel more and more confirmed in the belief that it would be indiscreet, not to say wrong, to abandon our tried friends and put ourselves into the hands of savages whose sole object too evidently is to obtain the few articles in our possession. We therefore gave Lorice to understand that we would remain where we were until the arrival of Queen Maria, she being daily expected from the north. He was disappointed and downcast at our answer, but at length left us with apparent good feeling.

Dec. 21. Lorice did not remove to-day according to his statement yesterday, but instead went out with a party on a hunt.

During the day we saw a great smoke at a distance northward, and our young chief says it is Queen Maria with her tribe, that she is coming down to the Strait, and that he will go to meet her to-morrow. Of course we rejoice in the tidings, and hope all will prove true, as this is what we have long waited for.

A young Indian brought us a pocket-knife to sharpen. We immediately recognized the knife as one which had been stolen from us, each of us having lost a knife of this description. We signified to the one who brought it that the knife was ours; but as we could not prove that he was the thief, nor find out the culprit, we permitted him to keep it.

Near sunset we witnessed a scene altogether novel to us. Nearly all the women in the camp assembled on a lawn and engaged in a game at ball-playing. They were noisy, lively, and energetic. At the close of the game an altercation took place between our Jezebel and another woman. A squabble ensued, when all the other women and many of the children arranged themselves in a large circle around the combatants. The scene ended without blood, but not without a torrent of angry and bitter words which continued until late in the evening. What was the cause of the contention we could not learn; whether it was a dispute about the game or a revival of the old party feud was not certain; but one thing was clear, that Jezebel was the exciting cause.

We retired late to rest, but the noise in the camp and the incessant barking of a hundred dogs prevented sleep till near morning.

Sunday, Dec. 22. Louis started early this morning to meet the tribe of Indians whose smoke we saw yesterday.

During his absence Captain Lorice and several of his party paid us frequent visits and urged us with renewed importunity to strike our tent and go with them to-day, as they were about to leave. He seemed unusually earnest and anxious, and we apprehend that his haste to leave to-day is occasioned by the near approach of a large party friendly to Louis. We again and again rejected his proposals, urging the same reasons we had given on former occasions. His clan packed their horses, mounted, and moved off, while he and a few others lingered behind as if unwilling to leave us. Several times he seemed on the point of departing, when he would again return and sit in our tent, urging us to go by all the motives he could present, by flattery, and by the offer of rewards. These not moving us, he would sit silent for a long time wrapt in a thoughtful mood.

We made him presents of several articles, as we had done before, with which he seemed pleased.

Near sunset we saw our friend Louis returning accompanied by three lads of, as we judge, the ages of ten, twelve, and fourteen years.

On his arrival Lorice mounted his horse and disappeared. Louis reported that he had met a large body of good Indians, and that they would all be here to-morrow, but that the queen was not with them. He appeared much pleased that the Lorice party had gone.

On his way home he had slain a large puma. He had no weapons but his bolas and knife, but with the help of a fierce pack of dogs and his own skill and prowess he succeeded in slaying this powerful animal. He gave us liberally of the booty, and we found the flesh not very tough and quite palatable.

CHAPTER VII.

THE GREAT CHIEF CONGO AND HIS CLAN.

Dec. 23. Our Indian friends arose early this morning to make ready for receiving the coming troop from the north, and the young chief went out to meet and to escort them into camp. About noon they began to arrive, and for hours they kept pouring in and pitching their tents around us.

As usual all the labor was performed by the squaws, while the men and children assembled in multitudes before our tent, gazing upon us with eager curiosity and smiling good-nature. The clan consists of several hundreds, and when mounted it looks like a straggling regiment. It is headed by a young man whom they call Congo, and to whom they give the title of " de capita le grande."

Soon after his arrival this grand captain came and introduced himself to us as the great chief of the tribe, and spent several hours with us. He is a splendid specimen of physical organization, about six feet three inches high, well formed and graceful in figure and movements. He has a mild, open countenance with an intellectual stamp, and full of kindness and good-nature. His manners are easy and natural, and one might at first sight take him for a half-civilized native.

He rides a splendid horse, and dressed in his skin leggins and rich fur mantle he makes a fine appearance for a Patagonian. He speaks many Spanish and some English words, and thinks himself quite a learned man, especially as he can count ten in English.

He told us that a large part of this tribe were with Santa Maria, and that they would be here in one moon.

He inquired of us about our country. Was it great? were there plenty of guanacos? How we came to Patagonia; how many moons we were on the water? How long we had been here; how long we would remain? What goods we had brought? Whether we were not great captains and owners of many vessels? And many such like questions. To all these inquiries we gave him truthful answers that seemed to satisfy and please him. He was also curious to know the English name of almost everything around. After a social interview he invited us to visit him at "de casa le grande"—the great house—and presenting his hand in all the apparent cordiality of civilized etiquette, he left us and returned to his own tent.

Besides the grand captain there are several inferior officers, whom they call "poco capetans," or little captains, but how either of these offices is filled or what are the distinctive powers of each we have not yet learned. To all appearance, the man who shows the most prowess in fighting, the greatest dexterity in hunting, and the largest amount of loquacity and self-assurance becomes, like Nimrod of old, a natural leader of his tribe, and the people look up to and follow him.

At the same time there is little appearance of rule or government among them. Most of these savages assume an air of boldness and independence, as if every man was born a king and had never been conquered or made to serve, and thus they sweep the plains like the Bedouins, and roam from the Straits of Magellan to the Rio Negro on the north and from the shores of the Atlantic to the western Andes. To one of these subordinates, Santa Rio, we were introduced. He speaks the Spanish language, and shows by his name that he has been with priests of the Catholic Church. Four years ago he was sent from the Falkland Islands, where he was then residing, by the governor of those islands to trade for horses. Since then he has remained with the Patagonians, taken a wife from among them, and seems to have cast in his lot with the tribe. He is quite inferior in his person, but has more intelligence and a greater degree of civilization than most of the Indians. He is dressed in pantaloons and shirt of English fabric, over which he wears the skin mantle.

Of him we made many inquiries about the country and people. He informed us that Queen Maria was at Port St. Julian, north of Santa Cruz, on the Atlantic coast, about twelve days' journey from the Strait, and that there were about one thousand Indians with her. He also told us that the Lorice clan belonged to another tribe, and was composed largely of Tierra del Fuegians; that they spoke a different dialect (a fact we had surmised), and that they usually avoided the northern tribes of horsemen, for fear of becoming enslaved. Captain Louis told us that when they heard of the approach of the great Congo they were afraid, and left our camp before his arrival.

Thus we now see "the good hand of our God upon us" in first putting us under the care of our friend Louis, and then in preventing us from yielding to the flattery and the earnest and repeated solicitations of Lorice and his party to go with them. Although this persistency on our part left us for a season with only one family of five persons, yet in the end it has connected us with this large and ruling tribe, which it is probable we should never have seen had we gone as we were urged to do.

This sojourn of Louis and his family with the more degraded clan of Lorice was, we are informed, occasioned by his taking a woman of that clan for a wife, who after the great quarrel left him and went off again with her own people.

Toward evening the two daughters of our aged chiefs came smiling to our tent to greet us. We had supposed that they had become attached to young Indians of the Lorice party and had left their parents and brothers forever. We understand they had been sent for during the day and brought back from their wanderings. During the afternoon several of the "little captains" came to introduce themselves or be introduced, and to have a friendly chat with us.

At twilight, after the Indians had retired to their tents, Louis came to advise us to gather much brush into our tent on the morrow, because, said he, "Much Ingus;" and as there is but very little brush, he feared we would be robbed of our supply. Thus his thoughtful and provident care is constantly exercised on our behalf.

All things now look bright and cheering, and in our connection with this large company we hope to increase our knowledge of the country, and of the numbers, character, and habits of its inhabitants. These facts once obtained we shall be ready to embrace the earliest opportunity to return to our country and report, agreeably with our instructions, in Boston. But as no provision has been made for a vessel to come for us, the time of our departure from this country is altogether uncertain : whether in a month, a year, or never is all unknown to us.

Dec. 24. On awaking this morning my ears were saluted by the crowing of a cock. The music excited such a thrill of delightful sensation, and awakened such pleasing associations, that for the moment I seemed transported back to the rural scenes of my native land, and I could hardly realize that we were surrounded by wild savages. On going out among the tents we find quite a number of fowls, all living in the cabins and thoroughly domesticated.

Many of this tribe have a few manufactured articles which they obtained from vessels that have passed through the Strait or anchored in ports on the Atlantic coast.

The Indians of this land are physically a noble race. They are tall, well formed, and strong. They are not, however, gigantic. None of them are over six feet six inches, and few of them will weigh over two hundred pounds; and there is not a large proportion of them that will measure over six feet in height. Owing to the nature of their food, their great exertions to procure their game, and their roaming habits, there is little tendency to obesity among them. I have seen taller and much larger men among Americans and Europeans than among Patagonians. We are inclined to estimate the average height of what are called by sailors the "Horse Indians," or the pampas tribes, at five feet ten inches, and their average weight at 170 pounds. We think the extravagant estimate so often made of the size of the Patagonians has arisen from seeing them standing, walking, or riding on the shore, wrapped in their immense mantles of skin with the wool on, and with the upper end of this mantle rising above the head like a hood.

Some strangers have estimated the height of these savages at nine or more feet, and it may not be improbable that some of them have indulged in a touch of romantic exaggeration. While some of the women are large and tall, the average height of the females is much less than that of the men. There are many hoary heads in this tribe, some of whom appear venerable. During the day a very aged man came to our tent-door, and observing us engaged in writing, he began to clamor loudly and rapidly as if it were something very bad. Our good old Indian mother, who was in an adjoining tent, hearing his angry tones, came speedily to our help and remonstrated with the old savage with great earnestness. In a few minutes came Louis and bent down by the side of the old man, who was squatted before our door, and in mild and persuasive tones labored to pacify him and to convince him that our writing was not bad. But the excited old man still continued to storm more vehemently than ever, and poor Louis, finding all his efforts to still his rage fruitless, came within the tent and seated himself close to us, as if determined to stand between us and harm. The noise without had aroused the Indians in the camp, and numbers came to see and hear what was the matter. Under these circumstances we thought it prudent to lay aside our writing, which having done, and having taken kind notice of the old man, offering him water to drink from our own cup, he became quiet and soon retired, to our no little satisfaction.

As we could not understand the old man's words, we tried to learn from Louis the cause of his rage. He gives us the impression that it was our writing, but why we cannot now comprehend. Doubtless it arises from some superstitious fear.

After the aged Indian had left us, Louis inquired how many hatchets we had, and advised us to present one to the old man, telling us that he was one of the captains and a good man. This advice seemed wise and timely, and to partake of the nature of the instructions of "Him who spake as never man spake," viz., "Do good to them that hate you." We therefore told him that the old *capitan* should have a hatchet tomorrow.

Another event to-day was the bringing of a sick man to our tent, to whom Mr. Arms gave medicine, and promised to visit him to-morrow.

Dec. 25. This morning our young friend brought the old growling captain of yesterday to receive the promised hatchet. He appeared much pleased with the gift. We also showed him some of our things, and tried to converse with him in a kind manner, when he became quite cheerful and apparently perfectly friendly. In this whole affair we admired the conduct of Louis. He exhibited so much mildness and gentleness, mingled with such respect for the aged captain, that, though an untaught heathen, we perceived that he was not wholly ignorant of the practical use of the maxim, "A soft answer turneth away wrath." Who taught him to "rise up before the hoary head and to honor the face of the old man"?

He certainly managed the case admirably, and for aught we know saved our lives, as a riot at one time seemed imminent. During the turmoil of yesterday the grand Captain Congo was present, but he did not interfere except to say a few words now and then, the purport of which we did not understand. It is a happy and providential circumstance for us that our friend Louis and the great captain are on terms of intimate friendship. They speak kindly of each other and appear like affectionate brothers.

It is also very evident that Louis has created a general impression in our favor throughout the camp. This is seen in the smiling faces of the savages, their frequent visits to our tent, their presents of venison, and the pleasant regard they show us. But we are still a riddle to them, and they often say that we are unlike any other white men they have seen.

Captain Congo has been with us much to-day, and conversed in his usual cheerful manner. His mind is very active, and he is exceedingly inquisitive. He plies us with numerous questions, and seems anxious to get information on many subjects. We long with yearning desire to communicate to him those great truths—those "things of God," of Christ, of the soul of man, of its destiny; things which "the natural eye hath not seen, and which have not entered into the heart of man," but which are revealed only by the Gospel through the divine Spirit. But we are shut up on these themes for want of a medium of communication.

Congo tells us that he and many of his men will set out to-morrow on a grand four days' hunt, and invites us to accompany him. This we decline lest the fierce riding and the hard lodging should be too severe for us, and lest our presence and lack of skill and prowess should prove a hindrance to their movements.

A certain old man by the name of Captain Chen visits us every day and converses—or tries to—with much good cheer. He speaks Spanish tolerably well, and seems happy in spending his time with us. He is usually the first man to visit us in the morning. He has been out to-day on a hunt, and returning this evening he rode up to our tent-door, calling out, "Ha! Americanas!" On going out, he presented us with two large hams of guanaco, and a liver. Soon after this, the old man who raged so yesterday rode up and gave us another fine piece of meat. Captain Louis followed with his liberal donation, so that now we are overstocked with meat.

Several men, complaining of bodily infirmities, visited us to-day and Mr. Arms administered to them. The Indians also crowd around us to get their spurs and knives sharpened, and to obtain needles inserted into wooden handles, like awls, for sewing their mantles and other work. They are very happy to avail themselves of our skill and kindness in teaching and assisting them in many little things, which please them and draw them around us. We are surrounded by them most of the time, except when we sleep.

Dec. 26. The day has been filled up with our usual round of duties: entertaining the savages, making little articles of use to them, distributing small presents, attending to the sick, etc.

At evening Captain Chen came and took a supper of meat and broth with us in the best American style we could command. While eating along came Captain Ben, the boisterous old man whom Louis pacified, and he also partook with us. Both seemed highly delighted with the attention shown them, often exclaiming in praise of the supper, "Much bono, much bono."

Suddenly there was a noisy rushing of the Indians from the camp to the plain at a little distance. Immediately our old Indian mother came to tell us the cause of the excitement, as she always does when things do not go regularly. By expressive gestures she gave us to understand that two men were fighting with clubs; but as the crowd which surrounded them was great, we could not see the combatants. No efforts seemed to be made on the part of the chiefs to separate the fighters, and they went on like two mad bulls to beat and bruise each other, till, bloody and weary, they desisted.

Just before sundown a young man whom we did not know came to our tent-door, and, sitting down in a crowd, he began a long and loud harangue, vociferating and gesticulating with great earnestness. What the matter was we could not tell, but there was no doubt about his being displeased with something, and probably with us. Perhaps it was because we had not shown him sufficient attention, as we were now told that he was one of their captains. Several of our aged friends were with us, and they occasionally said a few mild-toned words to the young orator, apparently to pacify him, and would then, turning to us, say, "You no malo, you bono; we bono, Ingus bono." At length he retired, and the day closed in peace. Captain Congo came to see us and introduced his father, a tall, venerable-looking old man with a very mild and cheery countenance.

Dec. 27. Old Captain Ben made us an early visit this morning, bringing as a present a small bundle of rock salt. Whether this was a product of

Patagonia or whether it was obtained from some ship we do not know. We have never seen the Indians use salt, and had supposed that they did not know the use of it, but Captain Congo tells us there is much of it in the camp. Old Ben looked so smiling when he presented the salt that we have rarely received a gift with more pleasure.

The grand hunt of four days was organized to-day. Towards noon the company moved off under the direction of the great captain and his subalterns, taking with them what they call their "poco casas"—little tents—made for temporary uses. Nearly all the sound men, together with many women to carry the tents and other necessary apparatus, have gone in the troop, while few remain behind except the old and infirm, the women and children, and a few lazy drones; so that we are in the stillness of an almost deserted camp. We do not, however, regret this, as it affords us a little relief from the confinement and fatigue occasioned by an incessant crowd of visitors from the time we rise in the morning till late in the evening.

Dec. 28. The morning passed without interruption. At noon many of the lazy and impudent

Indians gathered around us, among whom was a man whom we judge to be a Spaniard, from his appearance and from his knowledge of the Castilian language. On the day of his arrival he came and squatted before our tent, and listened to our conversation with Captain Santa Rio relative to the country, its inhabitants, etc., with eager attention and evident suspicion.

He was quite social to-day for a long time, but at length he began to inquire what goods we had, and commenced begging one thing after another with intolerable earnestness and rapidity. We thought not best to gratify his cupidity, and only gave him two needles fitted into handles for *hodling* (sewing). He seemed dissatisfied and began to talk rudely, using offensive and impure language. This is common among these savages, and yet our ears have never been offended by anything of the kind from Louis and his old father and mother. We ceased conversation with this rude man, and he remained mute in our tent until night.

Some young savages seeing our axe lying at the door, took it without permission and went off to a clump of bushes, and began to amuse themselves by cutting; but the good mother, ever watchful of our interests, went boldly to them, took the axe out of their hands, and restored it to us. This she did of her own accord without a word from us.

Sunday, Dec. 29. Both my companion and myself being indisposed, we closed our tent and received no visitors until afternoon. As soon as we opened, in came the old Spaniard and remained until dark, recounting his great poverty, reminding us of our vast wealth, and keeping up an incessant begging. He appears to be supremely indolent, and this is the cause of his poverty. While others are active in procuring food, or in making or mending mantles, he lounges in his cabin or wanders about begging of others.

Before night we heard a shout,—" Pigo! Pigo!" " Barko Americana,"—and on looking out thought we descried smoke in the direction of the Strait, towards which the Indians pointed, and where they were confident a vessel had entered. But as the leaders and most of the strong men were absent on the great hunt, they seemed disinclined to go down to the sea. They said, however, that if one of us would go to-morrow, they would furnish us a horse and guide.

Not a whisper has come to us from our own

country or from any other part of the world since we landed, on the 14th of November. We have thus far been as completely cut off from all communication with friends as if we were on another planet. Is it any wonder, then, that our hearts leap for joy at the prospect of hearing from, or of sending some word to, the absent loved ones? On the morrow, therefore, "if the Lord will," one of us will hasten to the Strait.

Dec. 30. Last night a heavy frost spread around us, blighting the flowers and touching the grasses. This seemed remarkable, as the mercury was at 73° yesterday noon and it is hot to-day. We arose early and aroused the Indian who promised yesterday to be the guide to the sea. He lingered about securing the horses, though still repeating his promises to go. At length we started him off, but after being gone a long time he returned without the horses. By the actions of the savages we began now to suspect that they were unwilling we should go, probably fearing that in the absence of the chiefs we would go on board a vessel and not return, though we assured them to the contrary. As they did not move to help us, we gave up our hopes and went to our work. Soon, however, the man brought up two animals and saddled them; this revived our hopes, which were only again to be dashed to the ground as we saw the Indian and his brother mount the horses and gallop off in another direction. Thus ended their promises, and thus our eager expectations failed.

During the day our thermometer, which was hanging outside of our tent, was stolen. The loss was reported to our vigilant and faithful mother. So, after we had retired for the night, she came and called at our door and delivered up the missing article, together with a lost hammer. This done, she went entirely around our tent tightening the cords, and seeing that nothing had slipped out from under it and that nothing was exposed to be stolen. She is our most resolute and faithful police, and to us she seems a godsend.

Dec. 31. The last day of this, to us, remarkable year.

The great Indian hunt is over, and, according to arrangement, the host of hunters, laden with spoil, returned to-day. According to promise before he left, Congo brings us six livers, and many others give us large pieces of guanaco, but rather sparingly of ostrich-meat, of which, on account of the fat, they are very fond. The returned hunters crowded around us, delighted to meet us again, and the grand captain inquired with interest about the smoke at Gregory's Bay, and whether a " barko Americana" were there. He proposed to go himself to the shore to-morrow, and invited one of us to accompany him ; but as we tell him the vessel has undoubtedly left before this time, he gives up the idea of going.

After a genial visit, he gave us the parting hand in a very affectionate manner, and returned to " le casa grande" for the night.

We have been hoping a way would open for us to proceed westward to the Andes, and that we might, if possible, reach the Pacific coast, or get among the Araucanian Indians south of Chili, but the chiefs shake their heads ominously at the idea, and say it is impossible.

So the year closes upon us, and we are here "shut up to faith," not knowing what may be the developments of the coming year.

Jan. 1, 1834. We salute each other with " a happy new year," while our thoughts turn to the dear friends in the land of our fathers. We are here among savages, shut out from all the tender and precious endearments and priceless privileges of social and Christian civilization. No whispers of sympathy come to us on the night air, no voice of love echoes along these everlasting mountains from the northern winter to the regions of southern summer. No white-winged messenger-bird comes over the wide waste of waters to tell us of our loved ones' welfare. No morning greetings and evening benedictions of "kith and kin" come to our ears. No voices arrest us but the harsh sounds of the savages, the neighing of horses and baying of dogs, the roar of winds, and the rush and rattle of rain and hail.

> "The sound of the church-going bell
> These valleys and hills never heard,"

nor are the savages charmed by the silent voices of the stars or the sweet harmony of the constellations. No light shines upon them from above. Even the bright orbs of heaven—sun, moon, and stars—are to them unknown and meaningless factors in the great framework of creation.

The Indians have spent this day as they do most of their days, in idleness and recreations. Ball-playing is their favorite amusement.

Captain Congo visited us, and proposed to remove the whole camp down to Gregory's Bay tomorrow.

Many of the petty chiefs are opposed to this, and say they will not go. So there is loud talk and much disputation among them, and Congo came in the evening to say the opposition was so strong that the removal would not take place. So we see that his will and his word are not absolute.

Jan. 2. Very early this morning the great chief informed us that the camp would remove to-day, but not to the sea-shore. We struck our tent at once, and prepared to decamp. The march began about 10 A.M., but it was 2 P.M. before the ground was cleared. When about to depart they raised a great smoke, as is usual with them on such occasions.

Our faithful friend Louis took special care for us; furnished us with saddle-horses and horses for our luggage, which he carefully packed and watched until it was safely deposited in our quarters at the new station. This removal brought us within about twelve miles, as we suppose, of the Strait. This looks as if the warm dispute of yesterday ended in a compromise to go part way to the shore rather than to remove quite to the bay.

The appearance of our camp when broken up and on the march is truly grotesque. Some two hundred strong men mounted for the chase, armed with spurs, bolas, and knife, and accompanied by dogs that we cannot number, lead the van, or deploy to the right or left as scouts, while a larger company of women and children, with tents, poles, furniture, and all they possess, brings up the rear; often moving in parallel lines along the several trails, and often extending for many miles over the plains. Their horses are sometimes so heavily laden as to fall under their burdens.

Several guanacos were taken on the way, and on our arrival at the camp-ground we were presented with a fine portion of meat. One Indian rode up to us on the road and gave us each a piece of roasted ostrich which he had taken *en route*. He afterwards gave us the skin of the bird.

Jan. 3. Our present location is pleasant. On our left is a range of low mountains, overlooking a broad extent of country, including the Magellan Strait and the distant and dim shores of Tierra del Fuego. In our rear is a hill to break the force of the wind, with an open champaign in front.

In the afternoon Louis and I rambled out and climbed the hill behind our camp to obtain the wide view it affords, and to gather some insipid wild berries which grow on its sides, and which the Indians call "yanker."

While on this hill we saw three large smoke-signals on the south side of the Strait, made by the Indians of Eastern Tierra del Fuego. On descending from the hill we descried a smoke in the direction of Cape Gregory, and our people said that other Indians had arrived there.

Just at dark one man on horseback came to the camp from that direction, and on his approach the Indians rushed out in great numbers to meet him.

It is reported that Queen Maria is advancing with a very large train, and our camp is all astir.

CHAPTER VIII.

ARRIVAL OF THE "QUEEN."

Jan. 4. Early this morning a large party of our tribe set off to meet the coming troop from the north.

About 11 A.M. a division of the approaching strangers appeared on a hill in sight of our encampment, and made a signal. Immediately there was a great rushing and shouting on our right, and on inquiring the cause, we were told that the Americans were coming. A few minutes of waiting, and we were saluted in the English tongue by strangers who proved to be two young sailors, named Henry Boruck and Harry Hassel. The former says he is from the city of New York, and landed here from the sealing vessel Tally, Captain Allen, of New London, Conn., May 20th, 1833. The latter says he hails from Washington, D. C., and left the schooner Elizabeth Jane, Captain Albertson, May 12th, 1833. Wild, thoughtless youths, they became dissatisfied with their situations on board their vessels, and resolved to run away and abandon themselves to the pleasures of savage life. But the poor fellows have "paid dear for their whistle," and they have learned their folly at a high price. They now rue the day when they left the society and comforts of civilized life and planted their feet on these savage shores. They say they have suffered bitterly, and have sometimes desired death rather than life. Their clothes have been taken from them, and Henry wears an old, greasy, and cast-off skin mantle; while poor Harry, less fortunate, has not been able to obtain even that apology for a garment, and vainly endeavors to cover his nakedness with the shadow of an old tattered monkey-jacket and the remnant of a pair of duck trousers in which he left his vessel. These are his only garments by day and night, and he has suffered greatly with the cold during the long winter. These men have been with the savages about eight months, and have been constantly roaming since the winter broke up, stopping only a few days in a place. They have been, as they say, a great distance to the north, sometimes camping on the sea-shore, sometimes advancing far into the interior. They have been with the division of Santa Maria, who is now on her way back to Gregory's Bay.

Yesterday an Indian of our tribe went out to meet them, and these young men, learning from him that two of their countrymen were here, left their company by stealth in the evening, and, travelling most of the night, arrived at our camp before noon to-day.

While all the Indians are mounted, these sailors are made to travel on foot with the dogs, and are often reproached with the name servant and slave. They are barefooted, and, being obliged to keep up with the horses on their journeyings over rough and smooth places, their feet are swollen, cracked, and sore. They are covered with dirt, and their beards have not been shaven or their hair cut since they came into the country. They are made to do the drudgery of the savages, such as catching their horses, leading them to water, gathering fagots, kindling their fires, roasting their meat, bringing their water, etc.

Instead of becoming chiefs and gratifying their baser passions at will, as they expected, they are deprived of every privilege, despised by the savages, and degraded to the most abject condition.

But although they now see their folly, they do

not reform their lives, but are constantly exerting a baleful influence upon the Indians, teaching them the use of the vilest words, and thus demoralizing, if possible, these degraded natives. They are awfully profane, and they have taught the Indians to take that sacred name of which they have no knowledge in vain, and to trifle with the God of whose attributes they have never heard. Almost every sentence which comes from their lips is uttered with an oath, and we are constantly rebuking them for a habit which to them is like breathing.

With all the roughness and profanity of these poor sailors, their misery makes them glad to see us, and they beg to remain under our care and protection, hoping that we may help them on board of some vessel and thus end their dreadful exile.

They excite our painful sympathy. We pity them, but we dread their influence on these savages; for it is in deadly opposition to that which we are endeavoring to exert.

In the afternoon another American youth of only sixteen years, named Nicholas Druery, came to our camp on horseback in company with an Indian with whom he lives. He hails from Westerloo, N. Y. This young man belonged to the schooner Transport, Captain Bray, of Bristol, R. I. The schooner was wrecked on Tierra del Fuego in March, 1833. The crew were all saved and taken off by the Unicorn, Captain Low. Nicholas, preferring a savage life, left the Unicorn at Gregory's Bay, and has been with the Indians ever since.

He tells us that there is a man named Daniel Smith, of New York, and also an Englishman and a Portuguese, who left their clan some time ago to search for a vessel in which they might leave the country. What had become of them, whether they had escaped or perished with hunger, or at the hands of the savages, he knew not. At evening Nicholas returned with his Indian master to the Queen's camp, which he judged was about twelve miles from here, while Henry and Harry remain with us.

Sabbath, Jan. 5. The Indians have been interchanging visits with the Queen's party during the day. We have not yet seen her Majesty, but one of us will probably go to her camp to-morrow. We are told that there are about five hundred Indians in her train. We learn also that many of these savages play at cards, which recreation they call *berrica*, and also at dice, which they call *terraci*. Ball-playing they call *sonkey*, and in this they have indulged largely to-day. Surely we have been preceded by missionaries in Patagonia, though not by ambassadors of the Lord Jesus. These poor, blind natives have not been told the story of redemption nor taught "the name which is above every name," except to profane it. They know nothing of the Sabbath of rest and peace—nothing of its elevating and soul-inspiring joys.

They have learned to swear and gamble, to smoke and drink, but they have unlearned none of their original sins.

About sunset our attention was turned to the tent of Santa Rio, the Spaniard, by groanings, rattlings, and strange noises. We went immediately to him, and found him complaining of sickness and great pain. An Indian doctor was sitting upon him, moaning, wailing, sucking his thumbs, striking his breast, blowing through his fists, sucking the eyebrows and face of his patient, blowing upon him, and rattling over his head two bags of dry skins, in the form of junk-bottles, in which were a large quantity of pebbles.

This ceremony was continued a long time,

until one would suppose that a well man would have fallen sick, and a sick man would have died.

By what we saw on this occasion we are led to think that these savages, like many of the more civilized races, believe in possession by evil spirits, and that these wild and superstitious measures are practised to exorcise them.

Jan. 6. The long-looked-for Patagonian Queen has at last arrived. She comes to us not in regal pomp and royal splendor, attended with a brilliant retinue of "peers of the realm," but as a savage squaw with a few straggling attendants, and escorted hither by Mr. Arms, who went up to her camp this morning.

Santa Maria is an aged woman, tall, large, and well formed, with a mild and somewhat intelligent face. She is partially civilized; has visited the Falkland Islands, and converses tolerably well in Spanish. She appears amiable in her disposition, and we are pleased with her. She is now living, as we are told, with her fourth husband, whose name is Kahatech. She has four sons, viz., Parpon, Toorloon, Checo, and Bistante. The oldest is a captain in the clan.

On entering our tent the Queen offered me her

hand with civility and kindness, and then introduced her husband, for whom she manifests much affection.

We prepared a dinner of boiled meat, and our royal guests partook with us in the best style we could offer. They seemed to relish the savory meat, and, as we furnished but one course, the dinner was soon despatched. Our conversation then turned on various subjects, and she inquired of us how long we would remain in her country, what goods we had brought, when there would be more vessels at the bay, etc., etc.

She also invited us, with great apparent cordiality, to go and live with her. This invitation we thought best to decline for the present, as we do not expect to find friends who will treat us with more kindness than the family of Louis.

On telling the Queen that I would visit her at her lodge in a few days, she insisted on my returning with her to-day and spending some time with her; and her importunity became so great that, after several excuses on my part, I assented to go with her at once, and made my preparations to leave.

We then presented her with a nice scarlet broadcloth cloak which we had made on board the Mary Jane on our voyage out. We also gave her a hatchet, several knives, thimbles, needles, etc., with which she seemed much gratified. She had detailed a fine horse for me, and we all mounted, and the cavalcade set out at near sundown for the royal camp. We found the distance not great, and as the summer twilight in this high latitude is prolonged, we arrived at the camp before it was ended. The Indians crowded around in great numbers to welcome their chief and to get a peep at the stranger.

I was invited immediately into the Queen's tent, which is larger than any of the others, but made and furnished in the same general style. It is occupied by several families in her train.

Santa Maria dresses in a mantle of skins, wears a few beads around her wrists, and when she rides out wears a pair of boots made of the skin of a horse's leg; but in none of her personal attire is she distinguished from a private individual. I supped with her and her husband on roast guanaco, and this ended, she prepared my bed of skins, and covered me with the care of a mother.

Jan. 7. On arising this morning the good old Queen brought me a piggin of water and a piece of soap to wash my hands and face. This was a novelty. It is the first time I have seen a Patagonian think of water to wash face or hands, or food or clothing.

After this ablution a good breakfast of boiled meat was provided, with salt to flavor it. After breakfast the old lady inquired how long I would stay, and when I told her that I must return to-day, she urged me to remain another night. She did all in her power to render my visit agreeable, and I have seldom been treated with more simple and genuine hospitality even in a civilized land. Finding that I could not be persuaded to remain over another night, she girded a horse for herself and another for me, and at 3 P.M. we set out, and she escorted me back to our encampment, rested there a while, and then returned to her own quarters.

As I was about to leave her tent she presented me with a new guanaco mantle made in the best manner, and finely painted. She also gave me seven hen's eggs from a hen which she kept in her wigwam with great care. A the time Mr. Arms visited her, she gave him a mantle made of lionskin, the only one of the kind in her possession. Among the Queen's household I saw a man whom the Indians call *padre*, and who acts as a kind of priest, though I cannot learn that he has any official duties to discharge except in burying the dead. The padre wears his hair and his mantle like the women, lives in celibacy, performs no hard labor, and is supported by others. All this, of course, comes from some former contact with the Catholics; it may be from intercourse with the Spaniards along the Rio Negro on the north, with an old and abandoned settlement at Port Desire, on the Atlantic coast, or another at Port Famine, within the Strait of Magellan. And it is not improbable that Santa Maria has been baptized by a Catholic priest, as her name would indicate.

As yet we have witnessed no death and no funeral rites among the savages, but we are told by some of Santa Maria's party that when a man dies he is buried in a small hole in the ground, the padre treading down the earth over him, and that then his horses and dogs are all killed, and his tent frame and covering, his mantles, lasso, bolas, skins, and all that pertains to him, are burned, no vestige of the man, or of any thing that he possessed in life, remaining.

On inquiry as to the marriage ceremony, we were told that the lover purchases a wife with a horse or horses of her father, and that the nuptials are celebrated by killing and eating a horse. Polygamy is common among the Patagonians, and husbands and wives have little regard for fidelity, and part at will.

CHAPTER IX.

SAIL HO!

Jan. 8. Some Indians ascended Table Mountain, near us, this morning, where they obtain an extensive view of the Strait, and returned with the report that a vessel was coming into the bay from the south-west. Immediately the whole camp was in commotion, and the loud cry of "Barko Americana! Barko Americana!" rang from tent to tent. Troops of savages were soon mounted on their horses, and galloping off at full speed to meet the coming stranger. Nothing seems to excite such jubilant feelings as the approach of a vessel to their shores, and I must confess that on this occasion my heart partook largely of the general joy, though my emotions were excited by very different motives from those of the crowd. They longed for tobacco, rum, and fire-arms; we longed for news from the civilized world, for news from home. Hope filled us with unutterable joy.

My companion mounted a horse and went down to the shore with the Indians, while I remained to guard the tent. At evening Mr. Arms returned and reported that the vessel was a French brig from Valparaiso, bound to Havre; that three of the American sailors who had so long been in Santa Maria's clan had succeeded in getting on board and shipping for France; and that the captain had received him very courteously, and kindly offered us a free passage in his brig: a generous offer, for which both we and our patrons and friends at home will ever thank him.

Thus the first vessel we have seen has come and gone without a letter or a paper from our dear country, or "a wish or a thought" from friends who are dear to us as life. This is tantalizing, but we bear it patiently, for it is one of the conditions of our mission to Patagonia.

"Though the vision tarry" we will wait for it, because it will come in due time. We are not prepared to leave this country as yet, even by the very favorable opportunity now offered us. We wish to meet other Indian tribes, if possible, and to learn more of the country and of the condition of its people, trusting that when our work shall have been done, the good Lord will send us a direct conveyance back to our country and friends. So we wait the will of our Master.

Jan. 9. We set out this morning before sunrise, to visit the French brig. Found multitudes of natives on the shore, where they had spent the night in the open air. As the wind was high and the sea rough, no boat was sent to the shore from the brig, and about 8 A.M. she was under sail and wafted out of the harbor. Just as her sails were being unfurled, two vessels were descried at a great distance coming in from the east. This caused shouts of transport among the Indians, and a new thrill of joy ran through my heart, for I said now surely we shall have tidings from the outer world, and from our native land. So we all sat down upon the banks of the Strait, determined to wait the arrival of these vessels. Wind and tide opposed the progress of the schooners, and they were long in beating up into the bay Meanwhile I wrote a pencil note to Mr. Arms, informing him of the approaching vessels and telling him not to be anxious for me, as it was probable I should be obliged to remain over night in order to communicate with them. This note I gave to an Indian, bidding him to speed with it to Mr. Arms. Off he went at full gallop and was soon out of sight.

It was almost sunset when the first schooner arrived and dropped her anchor within hailing distance from the shore. I at once hailed the vessel in English, and the captain sent his boat and brought me on board. I introduced myself and told him the cause of our visit to this country and our present condition among the Indians. I enquired for letters, papers and news, but he replied that he had no letters and no news, as he had been long at sea. He was from New Bedford, Mass. Soon the second schooner, the Peruvian, of Boston, came up and anchored outside of us, and I hailed her from the deck of the first. The captain invited me cordially to come on board the Peruvian, but as it was near night, the wind strong and the sea rough, it seemed imprudent to attempt boarding her. She was reported bound for the Society Islands, and the New Bedford vessel for the Sandwich Islands, carrying a cargo of New England rum.

Having had no bread and no vegetables for nearly two months, I asked the captain if he would sell us a few pounds of sea biscuit and a few other edibles. He replied that he had nothing to spare; that his voyage had been long and unfortunate, and that he must keep what provisions he had. I then suggested that he might desire to replenish his store of meat by trading a little with the Indians, of whom there were many on shore. To this he objected, saying he did not like the looks of these savages, and that he would have nothing to do with them. Finding my suggestions rebuffed, and being very hungry, having eaten nothing since sunrise, and thinking I might get some food among the savages on shore, I asked the captain if he would be so kind as to return me to the beach. To this he said no, for it was quite rough and he had taken in his boats for the night.

I then said, "Very well, I am on board, and if you will allow me to sleep on the transom and set me on shore in the morning, all will be right." So we went below to the cabin, where I hoped to see a table spread for supper. But as no table was laid I reasoned that all hands had eaten before I went on board; but the steward, for what reason I know not, on clearing off the supper table, had left a plate, with one pancake on it. Now we are forbidden to covet, but I found it hard to suppress my desire to eat that cake. Still I held back till near bed-time, trying hard to entertain the captain with conversation, especially on matters pertaining to his profession as a seaman and on my experiences of Patagonian life, hoping that my remarks on these experiences in the matter of eating would be rightly interpreted. At last forbearance seemed to cease to be a virtue, and I became desperate and burst out with "Captain, I am very hungry; I have eaten nothing since morning, and have eaten nothing made of flour for many weeks. I see a cake on your table and with your permission I would like to eat it." He gave his consent, and immediately called out, "Steward! here, bring on some grub; this man is hungry." In rushed the steward with a plate of "cold junk" (salt beef) and another of "hard-tack" (sea biscuit). The feast was sweeter to my taste than the best Thanksgiving dinner I ever ate, though it might have been sweeter still. I thanked the captain for my delicious repast and lay down on the transom for the night.

Jan. 10. Early this morning I awoke, and taking leave of the captain and the vessel, went on shore with the mate, mounted my horse, and with an Indian attendant sped over the plains to our little home, to breafast with Mr. Arms on hot soup and boiled guanaco.

Before leaving the beach, I saw the Peruvian under sail and seeking a safer anchorage about a mile further up the bay. Hundreds of Indians slept on the shore during the night, hoping to open a trade with the vessels, and there they will remain, though half starved, for a week, should the schooners remain so long.

Captain Congo put a new guanaco robe with a fine piece of venison into my hands, as I landed this morning, wishing me to send them as a present to the captain of the schooner in his name. This I did, committing them to the charge of the mate who returned with the boat to the vessel.

On board the New Bedford schooner yesterday, I met the three American sailors who had succeeded in getting off to the French brig the day before. The brig meeting this schooner coming into the bay, the master requested the captain of the American vessel to take these men, which he did. I found them divested of their Indian dress, washed, shaved, and comfortably clad in the attire of seamen. All this cleansing and clothing had been kindly done for them on board the French vessel, and their appearance was so much improved I did not recognize them at first, and when they addressed me by name I enquired where they had seen me. The poor fellows were much elated at the opportunity of leaving these now dreaded shores.

Jan. 11. The cry of "Barko!" again rang through the camp this morning; and Mr. Arms took horse and went down to the Strait. On his arrival he found the sail to be one of the schooners, which attempted to sail yesterday morning and was driven back by a strong head-wind.

The Queen and her party have all come down and pitched with us, so that we now have a camp of some 700 around us.

Last evening, about sunset, Captain Congo, with the large troop left at Gregory's Bay when I returned in the morning, came up from the sea in a remarkably jubilant mood. The Indian who headed the train had an empty flour-barrel before him, lying across the neck of his horse. On this cask he was drumming with great energy, and shouting, "Americana barko bono! Americana barko bono!" while the whole line of Indians joined in the refrain, shouting, laughing, and making the welkin ring with their jubilation.

We were sitting in our little tent and looking at the long line in "Indian file," when the drummer rode up in front of us, bent over and tossed like a quoit a sea-biscuit into our tent. Another and another followed and performed the same act, until we seemed in danger of a surfeit. We were surprised, and could in no wise account for this liberal shower of food, falling like manna from heaven. I had left a ship that morning without a piece of bread or a grain of rice in my pocket. How then had these savages succeeded in obtaining such a supply? It is a riddle which we cannot interpret. We can only thank the Lord for giving us, "without money and without price," that which we vainly sought with money, and which we would not have refused even at a dollar a pound.

We invited Captain Congo and the Spanish Indian into our tent to-day, to inquire more at length of them about the country and the people. These men tell us that they have travelled all over Patagonia, and their descriptions accorded so nearly with our maps that we were satisfied that they had seen what they reported. We first requested them to tell us what they knew of the Atlantic coast in going north from the Strait. They first mentioned a river and a harbor where vessels sometimes anchor, giving the number of days occupied by the Indians in reaching that place. This we conclude to be Port Gallegas. Next came Santa Cruz, which they named distinctly. After this, and in a given number of days, they reached the small river which flows into Port St. Julian. Next, after many days, they reached Port Desire, with its river of considerable volume, and the *débris* of its ancient fort and settlement, once occupied by the Spaniards. Further on they mentioned a great gulf, or a deep indenture of the coast, which must be St. George's Gulf. Still further north was another river of much water, which must be the Chuput, and after long ramblings, and fording of some smaller streams, they came in sight of the settlements in the region of the Rio Negro.

In going up the coast they described much zigzagging to avoid obstacles and to find fording places on the rivers. Their descriptions seemed credible in a remarkable degree, as they accorded so nearly with the map which was before us.

Having thus followed our guides along the Atlantic coast, where we had data and way-marks to detect errors, we next requested them to lead us through the interior, which, to all the world beside the Patagonian, is a *terra incognita,* **and a** land of romantic conjecture.

They assured us that they had explored all that region, that in some parts there was "much grass, much ostrich, much guanaco, much lion," with some other quadrupeds and a few birds. They also said that in one place there was a great salt desert, with here and there lakes and ponds of water, and we understood them to speak of regions of sand and of something which we suppose to be volcanic ashes and other plutonic products.

We then took them farther west, to the mountain ranges and spurs, inquiring if the Indians had ever gone to the bases and foot-hills of the great mountains. They assured us that they had, and that there were woodlands and swamps which they could not penetrate, that the mountains were high and rugged and bold, and that they were often covered with snow, so that horses could find no grass, and that Indus would be very cold and hungry and could not get over the mountains. All this they acted out with energetic gesticulation, so that we could not mistake them.

We then inquired as to the probable number of inhabitants in the whole country. Santa Rio says there are three nations inhabiting this land, speaking different languages and of different habits of life.

On the northern borders are what he called the Oucas tribe, numbering several thousands. These live in tents of skin like the southern clans, and are partly agricultural and partly nomadic. They have horned cattle, horses, and sheep, and they also cultivate the earth to some extent. Occasionally they remove to short distances to obtain grass for their cattle when it is exhausted near them.

South of this region he again speaks of the great desert as covered in some parts with thorns and prickly shrubs, so thick as to render travelling very tedious. Still further south is the nation with whom we live, occupying the open country from the Atlantic to the western hills, and south to the Magellan Strait. These are sometimes called the Santa Cruz nation, and number about a thousand. All these, he tells us, we have met except one clan of a few hundreds, who are still hunting far to the north. The other tribe is called the Port Famine tribe, few in number, a mixed and inferior race, mostly wanderers from Terra del Fuego. With this clan we may include all the miserable savages of Terra del Fuego and of the western coast of Patagonia.

This account of the inhabitants of this great and wild country, with its islands and smaller islets, may be approximately correct or it may be erroneous. I give it as received on the best authority we now have. But our data are few and our sources of information imperfect. If corrected by further researches we shall be glad.

About the immortality of the soul and the character of the future state, subjects which we brought forward in this conversation, we find their notions somewhat similar to those of the North American Indians. They believe in the existence of the soul after death, and in a distinction between the good and bad. When a good Indian dies they say he will go to a land where there is no night, no winter, no pain, and no death, but where there is constant sunshine and eternal beauty, and where all will be supplied with fine horses and with everything which the heart desires; but as there will be no hunger or thirst there will be no need of hunting and striving for food. When the bad Indian dies, they say he will descend deep to an evil land, filled with darkness and barrenness and thorns, where there is much fighting and sorrow.

We could not feel sure that these crude notions

of the future state, with its rewards and punishments, originated with the Patagonian savages. It seems more probable that they are the result of imperfect information on the Christian religion communicated to them by sailors or Spaniards with whom they have come in contact.

We could not find that they have any distinct notions of a Supreme Being who created and who sustains and governs all things. When we called their attention to tangible objects, as mountains, waters, the sun, moon, etc., and inquired who made all these things, their minds seemed utterly blank, as if it were a subject on which they had never bestowed a passing thought. As yet we have seen nothing which appeared like religious worship among them. One day, while riding out in company with Captain Louis, on coming to a clump of bushes he dismounted, and with his knife cut off a portion of his horse's mane, rolled it into a little wisp, dug a hole among the bushes and carefully buried it. He then remounted his horse and we rode on without explanation, so that I was left only to conjecture as to the meaning of the act.

On inquiring how they would like to have American teachers come and teach them to read and write, as we did, and to instruct them in all things useful and good, they seemed delighted with the idea, and said it was "much bono." And when we suggested the thought of building a large mission-house at Gregory's Bay, where their children might remain and be instructed while the parents roamed for sustenance for themselves and their horses, they became much animated with the subject, and said that the Indians would all leave their children with the Americans, and would come now and then to see them and bring them "much guanaco and much mantle."

They seemed very anxious to know if missionaries would be sent, and how many moons it would be before they would come; also whether they would build "casa grande"—a large tent—with many other things relating to the subject. Of course we could make them no definite promise, but we thought it well to put these questions in order to ascertain their minds with regard to them though they little understood their import, in order to have something to report to the friends of missions in the United States.

From our conversation with these chiefs to-day we despair of ever being able to reach the western coast by land in the vicinity of the peninsula of Tres Montes, and we can only wait the developments of Providence as to our future course.

Soon after this conversation our camp was again set in motion by the cry "Barko! Barko!" On inquiry we were assured that a vessel was coming in from the east. I therefore took a spy-glass, and mounting a horse with Captain Congo, ascended the hill behind our camp for observation. But as no vessel was to be seen from this point, we concluded that it was a false report, and Congo said on descending to the camp: "Ingus hablao much mentair"—Indians tell many lies.

Jan. 12. A memorable day. We were aroused early this morning by the Indians, who came to assure us that a vessel had actually come into the bay. On arising we found large numbers of the savages preparing to go down to the shore, and we therefore concluded, as it afterwards proved, that this was not a false alarm.

I mounted a horse already prepared for me, and with the great Congo and others rushed down to the bay. On our arrival we found that the vessel had not anchored, but was a considerable distance off and slowly approaching the harbor. With

Congo and a number of petty chiefs I then rode some distance up the shore to obtain a nearer view of the schooner. On approaching opposite us and seeing a troop of Indians on horseback, the British flag was displayed, a gun fired, the vessel hove to, and a boat lowered and headed for the shore. As the boat neared the land I hailed her in the English tongue, "Boat ahoy!"

A well dressed gentleman in the stern of the boat sprang to his feet as if a shell had exploded alongside, and called out, "*Who? What do I hear? My mother tongue in this strange land?*" I instantly introduced myself to the gentleman, and he as quickly returned the compliment, "H. Penny, of Liverpool, England, owner of the schooner Sappho and cargo, bound to Mazatlan, California." I invited him to beach the boat and come on shore. He inquired if it were safe to land among these wild savages, as he had heard that they were giants, very treacherous, and cannibals withal. Having assured him that there was no danger, the boat was brought to land and he leaped on shore. He then inquired earnestly as to our situation and life among this people, and I gave him the principal facts briefly. He remarked that as the vessel approached the bay they had descried a troop of Indians on horseback, and feeling a curiosity to get a nearer view of them, he had ordered his vessel to be hove to and a boat to be lowered that he might approach the shore cautiously to reconnoitre, not dreaming of finding men of his own race and tongue. He furthermore said he had brought several small presents in his boat to give him access to the savages in case he should deem it safe to land. On asking him what presents he had, he mentioned a box of raisins, some nuts, prunes, handkerchiefs, and a few bottles of rum or gin. These intoxicants I begged him to conceal, as their use by the savages would be sure to make trouble, and might end in the loss of our lives. To this request Mr. Penny assented readily, and leaving the bottles in the boat, he ordered the other articles to be brought on shore. He then wished me to distribute them among the Indians at my discretion, pressing a liberal share upon my companion and myself. I then seated all the Indians in ranks upon the grass, opened the packages and distributed to every one his due portion. The Indians laughed and shouted and fell to eating the fruits with gusto and many grunts, making altogether a grotesque scene.

Captain Congo then presented through me a nice guanaco robe to Mr. Penny, which was accepted with many expressions of gratitude. Meanwhile Mr. Penny invited me to go on board the Sappho, remarking, "You will be highly pleased with my captain; he is a missionary man, a good Christian, and a communicant of the Church of England." I cheerfully accepted the invitation and went on board. Mr. Penny introduced me to Captain M. M. Melward, of Liverpool, adding a few remarks on the object of our visit to Patagonia, and our state and circumstances among the Indians. The captain's reception was very cordial. He grasped my hand, and said, while tears started from his eyes, "My dear friend, what can I do for you? My ship's stores are at your disposal; command me what you will and you shall have it." His tenderness and generosity were very touching, and he showed himself at once all that Mr. Penny had declared him to be. He expressed a true interest and sympathy in our work, and assured me that it would be a pleasure to him if he could be of any service to us.

I was invited to lunch with him and Mr. Penny, and then urged to take liberally of the ship's stores, to carry up to our camp; but I declined taking anything considerable, as an abundance of edibles would excite the cupidity of the Indians and lead them to feel that they were no longer under obligations to feed us; and then we did not care to add much to our baggage; so I took a few sea-biscuits, a pound or two of salt pork, and, by the earnest recommendation of Mr. Penny, a few pounds of oatmeal to cook in our soup.

The day was not yet spent, nor even half of it. Our good friends expressing a wish to see our quarters in the camp, I invited them to accompany me thither, to which they readily assented. The schooner having been brought to a good anchorage, sails furled and everything made snug, we took boat for the shore, where the Indians had been accumulating for hours, to the number of several hundreds. Signifying our desire for horses, two were immediately offered to the owner and the captain, and we mounted and galloped off, a large troop of savages accompanying us with a multitude of dogs. Mr. Penny, who is young and elastic, and who has travelled among the American Indians in Mexico, California, and other parts, was a bold rider, greatly diverting the natives by his feats of skill, such as turning in his saddle and riding sidewise, first on one side, then on the other, then riding on his knees in the saddle, then standing upright on his feet, with other feats of agility. All this was done while our horses were on a full gallop and with the dexterity of a circus rider. Meanwhile Captain Melward kept close by my side, seeming a little nervous at the appearance of the rude natives. As they rushed this way and that, coming close to us with savage boldness, the captain drew closer to me and asked if these fellows were not treacherous. I assured him we had felt no fear while among them, though we were entirely in their power. At length we arrived at the camp; the strangers were introduced to Mr. Arms, and after a little conversation we invited them to dine with us, our frugal table having been spread with the production (not productions) of the country. In our humble canvas tent the merchant and traveller and the English navigator sat down with two obscure American missionaries to a Patagonian dinner, with the addition of sea-biscuit—a delicious luxury to us—just received from the schooner. The scene was not unworthy of a sketch-book.

The sympathies of the kind-hearted captain seemed much enlisted on our account. I heard him say to Mr. Penny in an undertone, " This is *too* hard."

With renewed expressions of kindness and assurances of desire to assist us to a greater extent than they had done, these friendly gentlemen bade us good-bye and left our tent in season to return to the Sappho before dark.

The experiences of the day have indeed been among the pleasantest of our sojourn in this land.

Jan. 13. About ten o'clock last evening, after we had retired, some one called at our tent door for admittance. We immediately arose, and lo! Mr. Penny had returned and was calling for shelter and lodging. On entering our tent he informed us that when they reached the shore the wind was so boisterous and the sea ran so high that he feared to venture out in the boat, and proposed to remain on land till after sunset, supposing that the wind would then abate. But the captain, fearing for the safety of his vessel, had succeeded with no little risk in getting on board.

There was, however, no abatement of the wind, and as the sea increased its rage the boat could not return for him. He must spend the night in the open air, with the prospect of a storm before morning, or seek to reach the shelter of our tent. He had no horse and no guide at command, and for a time was unable to persuade an Indian to bring him up to us. At length, however, for a considerable compensation, a sturdy savage consented to take him behind him on his horse and bring him up. Two other Indians kept them company. On the way the guide left the main trail and turned aside to a clump of bushes. Here he dismounted, ordered Mr. Penny to dismount, and then began an attempt to rifle his pockets. Mr. Penny was alarmed, and urged the Indian to remount and proceed, but he was stubborn, and seemed determined to possess himself of a brace of pistols which he felt in his pockets. Mr. Penny kept his hands on them, and finally succeeded in satisfying the man with several other articles, especially his silk pocket handkerchief, which having made into a rude turban, he bound it upon his bushy head, remounted his horse, took the Liverpool merchant up behind him, and brought him safely to our door.

It is fortunate that Mr. Penny did not attempt to use his pistols in this unhappy moment of excitement. Had he done so, instead of proving a protection, they would undoubtedly have cost him his life. Had he dispatched this savage, there were two more near by, who were no doubt watching the affair in the dark, and who would have avenged the act instantly; or even had he succeeded in dispatching them all, he would have been left alone and helpless in the night and in the wilderness, with no one to guide him back to his vessel or forward to our camp, and on the next day he would have been sure to fall into the hands of the savages.

And just here it may be proper to remark that from personal experience, observation, and reflection, I have been led to the firm conviction that carrying weapons, whether at home or abroad, whether travelling in civilized or savage countries, is seldom a protection of life, but the contrary. Among savages the armed man is watched, suspected, feared, and this jealous fear often provokes attack. As with nations, so with individuals, arming on one side leads to arming on the other side, suspicion excites suspicion, fear awakens fear, and intimidation provokes intimidation, until blow responds to blow, and there is war in the wigwam, in the camp, and in the field.

When selecting an outfit in Boston and New York, some of our kindest friends advised us to take arms as protectors in times of emergency and danger. This counsel we rejected and went unarmed, and as unprotected as children. And this weakness we believe to be our strength. This defenceless condition is our defence. This lack of fire-arms is as " a wall of fire round about us."

But to return to our guest. We were truly glad to receive Mr. Penny again to our quarters, small and simple as they were, for though he was brave and cheerful, his situation was very uncomfortable. The night was gloomy, the wind blew, the clouds thickened and darkened, and a great storm was impending. He was separated from his vessel and captain, not knowing what would befall them, and utterly unable at this time to get on board.

In a short time after his arrival the rain fell in torrents and the night gathered blackness. Had we not been partly protected by the hills behind us from the careering winds our tent would probably have been blown down, leaving us exposed to the storm. As it was we were kindly shielded. The storm has raged on through the day, so that there was no going out till late in the afternoon, and Mr. Penny was shut up with us until 6 P. M. The rain and wind now so far abated that he proposed, though late in the day, to return to the

Strait and make another attempt to go on board. Accordingly horses were made ready, and my companion, attended by an Indian guide, accompanied him to the shore.

At dark a messenger came to our tent with our saddles and bridles, and informed me that Mr. Arms had sent back the horses which he and Mr. Penny had ridden down, and that he would sleep on board the schooner.

A large number of our Indians remain on the shore notwithstanding the storm, exposed day and night to the rain and cold, and half starved withal, all for the hope of obtaining rum and tobacco. The bare hope of getting a plug of the weed or a bottle of the fire-water would keep them on the beach, I believe, till they had well nigh perished from exposure.

Captain Congo returned to the camp this evening looking downcast and disconcerted. He was on board the Sappho all last night and most of to-day, and he was terribly sea-sick. He appears gloomy and cross, as if some strange thing had happened to him; he complains of the vessel and all on board.

Jan. 14. The rain continued to fall heavily during the night and for some time this morning.

This has been much the severest storm we have had since our arrival in the country, and it has rendered our fragile habitation somewhat uncomfortable. We saw the Sappho beating out of the bay this forenoon, she having been delayed two days through my invitation to the captain and owner to visit our lodge.

Near noon Mr. Arms returned, bringing a box of raisins, which Mr. Penny urged us to accept. On his arrival he told me that, in going down to the beach last evening, they met Congo with his train returning to the camp, that the chief seized Mr. Penny's horse by the reins in great anger, and threatened to take it from under him. Mr. Penny was now a prisoner, and Congo refused to let him go until he had promised to return the guanaco robe he had presented him, and also to give him a number of articles which he specified from his vessel. The late independent English merchant was now fast in the grip of a Patagonian savage, with no alternative but to comply with his conditions.

This base conduct on the part of Congo was occasioned by his dissatisfaction at not receiving as liberal a supply of tobacco as he wanted, and which he expected in return for the mantle he had presented to Mr. Penny. It so happened that there was no tobacco in the cargo of the Sappho except in the form of cigars, but these, though offered freely, would not satisfy him. He must have tobacco in plugs or the return of the robe. This Mr. Penny promised to return by Mr. Arms, together with various other articles to please the chief. This arrangement being concluded, Congo released his prisoner to go on his way. But his wrath had been much inflamed, for in addition to his failure to get the tobacco he had been roughly handled by the Sappho for twenty-four hours. It was pitch, jerk, plunge, roll, all night long and nearly all day, without regard to his chiefship. It was humiliating to his dignity and it stirred up his bile. So he cursed the bark, captain, crew, and all the English.

As we had several good mantles in our tent, Mr. Arms, on his return this morning, refused to take Mr. Penny's from him, promising to give Congo one of ours and to see that he was satisfied. This he attempted to do, but the chief was dissatisfied and sullen, and no explanation would conciliate his feelings. He utterly refused to take the mantle or anything else as an equivalent, and complained of the schooner as "malo" and the

English as "liars." Thus we were in trouble, and darker clouds than those of the storm seemed gathering around us.

It was hard to make the savages see that there was no lie on the part of the Englishman, or that we were not accomplices in a plot to deceive and cajole them.

As the debate went on the Indians came out of their wigwams in numbers and became noisy, some taking one side and some the other. At this point we thought it prudent to retire and remain silent, committing the disposal of the case into the hands of Him who restrains the wrath of man. We had done all we could to explain, to soothe, and to satisfy, and we quietly awaited the events which might follow.

The Indians had a long and noisy debate, and then all was still. The parties had retired to their lodges, and we were quiet until near night. Before sundown Congo came to see us with a changed countenance. His feelings were much softened, and he now entered into a familiar and pleasant conversation as aforetime, and finally listened to an explanation of the whole matter with calmness, and quietly received the mantle which had been offered him.

As his temper had been greatly irritated by the rolling of the vessel and his sickness, we told him that the schooner was not in fault, because the water made her roll. He replied, "Then the water is malo." "No," we rejoined, "the water cannot keep still because the wind agitates it." "Then," said he, "the wind is malo;" and here the matter rested.

This is but an example of the darkness of the savage mind. So ignorant and so infatuated are these savages that, as we have been told, when the wind blows strongly from the wrong direction they will take swords and knives and go out to fight it.

Just at dark our friend Louis came quietly and cautioned us to make all as secure as possible, to remove our effects to the centre of the tent and watch them, as he said he had heard some of the Indians " hablao malo"—talk bad—and say they will come in the night, cut through our tent with their knives, and rob us of our goods. This he illustrated by earnest gestures and by drawing his knife down the canvas. But we say with the Psalmist, " I will both lay me down in peace and sleep, for thou, Lord, only makest me to dwell in safety."

CHAPTER X.

CAMP LIFE.

Jan. 15. The rain continued all last night and till late this morning, when the clouds cleared away and the sun came forth to cheer us again, but the wind is still strong and piercing. Mr. Arms and myself are indisposed, so that we have kept our tent closed and have done little during the day. This may be occasioned in part by the excitement arising from the arrival of the Sappho with the connected events, together with the drenching storm which rendered our dwelling wet and uncomfortable. All is quiet again and we return to our normal Patagonian life, which, for the most part, is monotonous.

Jan. 16. By the aid of Santa Rio we have endeavored to get the census of the whole Santa Cruz tribe, and have, as we suppose, succeeded approximately. He makes the number to be about 700, but this estimate cannot be wholly reliable, owing to his ignorance and our want of ability to communicate satisfactorily with him. We think, however, that the number will not exceed 1000.

The tribe on the northern pampas is undoubtedly much larger, while it is, as we are situated, utterly impossible for us to estimate the Port Famine tribe, including the Fuegians and a few miserable Indians scattered along the western coast.

We perceive an ill feeling between the two large clans that have lately met. Captain Congo says that Santa Maria is "much malo," and he labors to excite our prejudice against her. And Maria says that Congo is a great liar, which is undoubtedly true not of him alone but of most of the tribe as well. These mutual jealousies and envyings between the leaders of the clans may lead to open rupture and the separation of the parties.

As among all the races of men, so among these dark-souled savages, envy and ambition are ruling passions. Those who seem to hold a "little brief authority" strive hard to show their importance and to persuade all around them to acknowledge their superiority.

Congo now appears to be an artful and insinuating flatterer, and his influence is on the increase, while that of Maria is waning. Doubtless this arises, in part at least, from the fact that he is young and vigorous and active, with a fine figure and a bold bearing, while, on the other hand, Santa Maria is advanced in life, of less fascinating address, and less activity and prowess.

As for the multitude of the Indians, their minds are fickle and inconstant as the winds, and he whom their capricious dotage exalts to-day may be execrated and abandoned to-morrow.

I went to-day to a tent and found a company playing cards. They had a full pack of English cards and appeared to play a regular game. This diversion was introduced among them by sailors together with other kinds of gambling. They swear, too; and we often hear shocking imprecations of damnation upon the head of some one. The first English sentence which I heard one of these savages utter was an oath, and I blush for my country and for the Christian name that through them this people have, first of all, been taught to blaspheme the Christian's God.

Jan. 17. We have conversed freely of late about leaving the country so soon as a suitable oppor-

ity shall offer. The object for which we came
ier has, so far as we can see, been accomplished,
I should the Lord open the way, we are pre-
ed to return and report to the Prudential Com-
tee of the A. B. C. F. M. on the state of Pata-
iia, the supposed number, character, habits,
l modes of life of the inhabitants, and whatever
y influence the determination of the Board as
endeavoring to establish a Christian mission in
s country or the contrary.

Most of the strong Indians went off this morn-
 on a grand hunt, accompanied as usual by
ny women and children, who carry the small
ts and take care of the game.

We went out to see the process of weaving
ong this people. We saw in the loom a piece
iigned for a blanket, and the weaver plying her
de. The loom is constructed by setting two
right posts in the ground, and fastening two
rizontal poles on these posts, one above the
ier, at a distance equal to the intended length
the blanket, which in this case was four feet and
alf. To these poles the warp is tied at each
l. The process of weaving is slow and tedious.
e weft is wound on a smooth pin or stick for a
ihin. The weaver seats herself on the ground

in front of the loom, and with another stick separates the threads of the warp for about six inches, and then, with the filling tied to an ostrich-quill as a shuttle, she passes it through the opened space. The stick is then drawn out, after serving the purpose of a lathe, and the warp is again separated as before. This process is continued until the blanket is completed, which is not until after many long and weary days, the artisan finishing fewer inches in a day than a hand-weaver would yards with the modern shuttle.

But, although the process is slow, the workmanship is marvellous. Many tints and a great variety of figures are wrought into the texture. These figures are often tasteful, and show much native genius in the operator. Where and how did these savages get this skill and taste? The yarn of which these blankets are made is spun from the wool of the guanaco. The fibre is long and soft. It is drawn out by the fingers, and twisted by means of a reed held in one hand. It is colored with various kinds of ochre procured back in the country. With these ochres the squaws also paint the guanaco robes, often with tasteful figures.

Queen Maria made us a long visit to-day. We

feel grieved at the quarrel between her and Captain Congo. The enmity still continues. When she left, she went into a tent quite near us, and we soon heard loud talk there among the women. This attracted attention, and the women came rushing in from all quarters of the camp, either to look and listen or to take part in the strife. Loud and angry words were uttered, which were soon followed by the tug of war, if we might judge from the reeling and rocking of the tent. As the rear of the wigwam was towards us, and as we did not feel disposed to witness the spectacle, we do not know who were the combatants or what was the occasion of the quarrel.

Three pleasant-looking boys have for several days supplied us with two kinds of dry mountain berries, which they call "yanker" and "porton." With these little presents they plead eloquently, and almost irresistibly, to be admitted into our tent, a privilege which we long to grant them freely, but are often unable to on account of the great crowd of the older folks who press in upon us. We feel sorrowful to think that these bright-eyed and smiling boys and girls must grow up to manhood and womanhood in darkness. In darkness they live, and in darkness they must die.

Jan. 18. The great hunting-party returned late last evening with much game, and most of the night was spent in roasting, eating, singing, shouting, and carousal.

We retired late, and were just falling into sleep when a large body of the savages came like a rushing tempest, with what seemed like a war-whoop, and surrounded our tent in a close circle. They stood silent for a moment, and then began to talk in an undertone around the circle. The moon was then in her first quarter, and it was so light that we could see the circle and the forms of the savages. We arose and looked out of our tent-door through a crevice, watching them from within, while they could not see us. Their low talk, sometimes sinking to a whisper, continued ten or fifteen minutes, and then suddenly, with another whoop, the ring broke and they all scattered.

What their object was in paying us this nocturnal visit we cannot now understand—whether in their glee to honor us in a savage serenade, or to kill and rob us in their savage cupidity, we know not.

The movement was mysterious, and at first startling, but it passed off quietly, and we re-

ned to our pallet and slept peacefully until
)rning.

The Indians have kept us busy as artisans much
the day, in making spurs and *hodles* for them
d in sharpening their knives.

Jan. 19. This has been one of our most quiet
ndays. Our tent has been left partly open, so
at the natives could look in upon us, but we
ve admitted none of them within, not feeling
le to converse with them intelligently on the
important theme, and choosing therefore to
end to our devotions in a quiet manner.
Several of the Indians brought us little jobs of
rk, but we satisfied them by telling them that
would attend to their requests to-morrow.
me have been engaged in hunting, some in
rmandizing and sleeping, and some in gam-
ng. They play for wagers, and the other day
iaw a good pair of shoes staked against three
igs of tobacco. The Indian doctor has been
;aged most of the day in different parts of the
np, moaning, screaming, blowing, shaking his
tle-bags, and going through all his incantations.
ich confidence seems to be placed in his round
ceremonies; for he is employed by all who are
from the chief captain down to the meanest

individual. They not only believe that his rattling incantations can drive possession from the human body, but also from dumb animals. He was engaged to-day at the tent of Congo in exorcising evil spirits from a sick horse. The usual process was gone through with, excepting the rattles, which were omitted, doubtless wisely, as they might have been received with less patience by a dumb beast than by a savage.

Every day gives us fresh illustrations of the dark character of this people, but our pain is that we cannot appeal to their understanding and their hearts.

Jan. 20. Several of the clan have taken their all to-day and gone northward, and Captain Congo informs us that he and most of the camp will remove to-morrow, a small party only remaining on the ground. They invite us to go with them, but as we have decided to leave the country by the first opportunity we choose to remain with our steadfast friend Louis and a hundred, more or less, of the Indians, in order to be within reach of the Strait should a vessel come that might take us off. Should we now retire far into the interior there would be no hope of our getting away, however many vessels might pass through the Strait. It affords us pleasure to find that Louis and a small party will remain to feed and protect us, while the great body of the tribe go north. In fact we had nearly resolved to stay, even if left alone and with means of subsistence only for a short period, as the object of our visit to Patagonia is accomplished, and we wait only for some conveyance to another field if it be the will of the Lord.

Jan. 21. Our sleep was interrupted again last night by the tremendous racket of the old doctor, who continued his medicinal noises until near morning, breaking out, from time to time, in strains of unusual energy and fierceness, as if he had really got the devil by his horns at last.

Early this morning the Indians prepared to decamp. Captain Congo bade us good-by and led off a host on horseback. Queen Maria and Louis remain, and we are told that only eighteen horses are left to our party.

An Indian whom we call Captain John handed us an English Testament to-day. It is probably one left behind by one of the American sailors, who considered it a burden. Probably there are few dark places of the earth where copies of the sacred Scriptures are not scattered, but where they shed no light for want of readers.

We had a conversation with Santa Maria on the subject of a Christian mission here. She seemed pleased with the idea of Americans coming to live with the Indians to teach them good things, but did not favor their building a house and remaining stationary. She thought they should travel over the country with the clans and thus instruct them.

In the afternoon a thunder-shower swept over us. This is the first we have seen in this land. We have heard light and distant thunder before, but have had nothing like a regular shower until to-day.

The thunder caused a great barking and howling among the dogs, but there was no unusual excitement among the Indians. After the shower the savages killed a horse and distributed it among all the tents. All then fell to roasting and eating, attended with much apparent joy and hilarity. Was it a marriage-feast, or was it an offering to the "unknown God" of thunder? We could not know.

Jan. 22. Several more families have left us to-day, and followed the party that went north yesterday.

Those who remain have spent the day in feats

of gormandizing beyond anything we have before seen. Large pots have been kept on fires from morning till night, and the Indians have gathered around them, feeding the fires with fagots and dry grass, and constantly consuming and renewing the contents. Scarcely a piece of the horse slaughtered yesterday remains in the camp.

Intelligence was brought us to-day from the Lorice party. This is the first news we have had from them since they left us. The report says that two of their number have died since they parted from us, and that two others are sick.

We were also informed that the three sailors who left Maria's clan some time ago—viz., an Englishman, an American, and a Portuguese—are with this clan. As Captain Congo has left, and as our party is now small, we are told that Lorice and his Jezebel will soon pay us another visit. It is said that they are not far off. Well, let them come if they must, but we have no desire to see that Amazon again.

We had another thunder-storm this afternoon, with a fall of large hailstones.

Jan. 23. The Indians returned from their hunt to-day with very little game. So the gluttony of yesterday is succeeded by fasting and hunger.

Checks, balances, and compensations seem to act in savage as in civilized lands.

About noon we were told that a vessel was coming up from the west, and shortly after a sturdy Indian came to our tent bringing a pale and sick white man behind him. This young man introduced himself as William Marshall Thornham, of Hull, England, aged twenty years. He said that he ran away from his vessel with two other sailors about a year ago, and that they all vowed to keep together and never forsake one another, come what would. Since then they had roamed with the Indians continually, suffering hunger and hardships almost unto death, being obliged to tramp on foot, without shoes, often over dry stubble, sometimes among flinty pebbles, then over sand-hills, and again among thistles. His feet were badly cracked, lacerated, and swollen; his hair was dishevelled, his face begrimed, and he had no clothing except an old, tattered, dirty, and cast-off skin mantle. A few weeks ago, coming in the proximity of the Strait, he and his two companions, in a fit of desperation, ran away from the clan with which they had travelled. They then wandered along the shore of the Strait, living upon mussels and watching for a vessel in which to get away. Soon afterward, falling in with a clan of the Port Famine tribe, they were made captives and treated with cruelty. William stated that if they attempted to get away from the clan, they were threatened with death by having arrows pointed at them. At length a vessel had anchored near them, and his two companions by a dexterous effort had eluded their captors and succeeded in getting on board the schooner, leaving him in his enfeebled state to the mercy of the savages..

The exasperated Indians then kept up a sharper watch over him than before. If he went a little distance from the camp, they would suspect him of designing to run away; when they would bring him back, and pass their knives across his throat as a sign of his fate should he attempt to get away. They next stopped his rations in order to weaken him so that he could not run, and he told us that for four days he had eaten nothing except a few watery and insipid berries which he found near the camp. Once or twice when Indians were all out of the tent, and when they supposed him to be asleep, he crawled around the tent and found a small piece of meat which he attempted to eat, but before he had swallowed a mite in came a savage and tore it from his teeth, and with a dark frown drew his knife across his throat. Soon a painful bowel complaint came on, and the poor man was unable to walk, and came near death. In this state some of our tribe found him, took him from the Yammerschooners (beggars), as this mongrel tribe is called by sailors, and brought him on horseback to us.

His appearance is truly distressing: emaciated and heart-broken, forsaken by the companions who had vowed to stand by him in weal or woe, to live or die with him, he is an object to excite our deepest sympathy and compassion. Even our Indians seem to pity him, and they delivered him up to us without remonstrance. We immediately took him into our tent, prepared the best we had—warm broth—for him, then bathed him in warm water, and dressed him in a suit of clothes, while Mr. Arms took him as his patient, administering carefully to his case. We endeavor to cheer him by assuring him that we will do all in our power to help him and to get him out of the country, should we find an opportunity to go ourselves.

He says it is true that a schooner named the Macdonald, Captain Clift, brother to the captain

William Clift with whom we came out in the Mary Jane, anchored far west of Gregory's Bay; that his companions got on board of her, and that he had heard that Captain Clift would anchor in Gregory's Bay and take us off. This was joyful tidings, and we determined at once that Mr. Arms should go down to the bay and learn what were the facts in the case. Accordingly he went, but returned with the report that no sail was in sight. This was a damper; for our hopes had been raised to a high point, and the disappointment was not small. William felt it even more keenly than we did, for he had a desperate desire to get out of the reach of those by whom he had suffered so much, and now the poor youth almost sank in despair.

But we are more accustomed to these alternations of hope and disappointment. We are in the Lord's hands, and there is nothing better than to wait his will.

Mr. Arms said that on reaching the bay he found the wind and current favorable, and there was no doubt that Captain Clift had gone on without stopping for us.

Young Thornham tells us that he left parents in Hull, and that he has now been absent from

England four years, having left at the age of sixteen.

He says he was persuaded to run away in Patagonia by older companions who told him that he would have plenty to eat, a good horse to ride, no work to do, and every indulgence the heart desired; that he would, in fact, be a chief, and live as he pleased. Thus the poor fellow was beguiled to his cost, and his experience has been bitter. He seems a pleasant and amiable young man. He is modest and respectful and uses no profane or vile language. The contrast between him and other sailors whom we have met here is very striking.

Jan. 24. Several of our Indians went down to the shore early this morning to see if the schooner reported yesterday had not come in during the night, but they returned with the word that she had gone on without anchoring.

Yesterday the Indians said that the whole camp would go down to the Strait to-day, and their horses were brought up this morning for the purpose; but on hearing that the vessel had gone on they seemed disappointed and displeased, and determined to stay at home. So all was quiet again, and we retired to our little tabernacle to read and write. While thus busied in our work the Indians had, unconsciously to us, taken their horses and moved off stealthily. Some time in the afternoon we were surprised, on looking out over the camp, to find nearly all of the vigorous men and women gone, including our trusty friend Louis. On inquiring what this meant, we were told that the Indians had gone off on a hunt. This seemed incredible, especially as they always told us when they were going hunting. Looking all around, we noticed a few of the last stragglers of the camp moving towards the sea, but no one going north in the direction of the hunting-grounds. As we shook our heads and looked incredulous, the savages then said that their companions had not gone for guanacos, but that they had seen a drove of ostriches among the sand-dunes, lying between us and the Strait, and had gone in pursuit of them. Neither could we credit this; and as their movements and language indicated duplicity, we began to suspect that they had seen a vessel, and knowing, for we had told them, our intention to leave them by the first opportunity, they had slipped off thus slyly, intending to deceive us and keep us with them.

While we were thus conversing and looking towards the Strait—not, however, expecting to see a vessel, as we could not see the water without ascending a hill in our rear—all at once I descried the topgallant sail of a schooner through a small notch in the table-land lying between us and the sea! The riddle was now solved; our suspicions were true. The troop had gone off secretly, having seen the vessel, not intending to let us know it or to give us a chance to reach the shore.

We asked at once for a horse, but for the first time were met with a flat denial. One and another replied to our repeated calls, "*No hos you.*" But we were determined one of us should go down even if he went on foot. At last an old woman, who had always been kind to us, brought us her horse, for which we had promised a liberal compensation. We had never before been obliged to hire a horse. Mr. Arms mounted and set off, while I remained to make any preparations that could be made in anticipation of leaving. In the evening he returned with the report that the schooner Antarctic, of New York, Captain James S. Nash, of Rhode Island, had anchored in the bay, and that the captain would take us on board to-morrow, requesting us to be down at the sea at 9 A.M.

Mr. Arms found Louis on the shore; he had

used the same deceit as the other Indians. By urging, however, he persuaded him and a few others to return to the camp with him, and to furnish us with horses in the morning.

Things, however, still look dark and suspicious; the faces of some whom we have esteemed our most tried friends are changed, and we are not without apprehensions that trials await us before we can get out of the country.

William Thornham is exceedingly anxious lest we shall get off and leave him. He begs us not to forsake him, as this would blot out his last ray of hope for escaping from this terrible land, and leave him to die without a friend. We assure him we will not leave him behind if it is possible for us to take him with us, and that we will do for him as for ourselves.

CHAPTER XI.

FAREWELL TO PATAGONIA.

Jan 25. We spent most of last night in overhauling our goods, deciding what to take with us and what to give to the Indians, and in packing. A little before day we lay down and obtained about an hours rest. We rose at daylight, went to Louis's tent and aroused him to get up the horses. He was sleeping soundly, but on awaking him he grunted, rolled over, and told his young brother to go for them. We then returned to our tent, offered our morning prayers, ate a hasty breakfast, saw our luggage all in readiness, and assisted William in his preparations. But up to this time not a horse or an Indian was to be seen. Again we went to Louis, and found him fast asleep. We aroused and urged him to help us, and again he told his brother to go for the horses. Then again we waited, growing almost desperate at the delay. After two hours we saw a man leading up several horses, and our hopes revived. One of these was tied near Louis's tent, and we had our luggage brought out to be packed; but when our backs were turned the hitched horse was let loose, and in a trice all were out of sight. The snare was now too visible. The savages meant to keep us, and they were thus trying to consume time until the vessel should sail without us.

We now appealed to their cupidity. We told them we had many things to leave, saddles, bridles, axes, tools, clothes, etc., and that those who befriended us should have a liberal share. This proved the motor; these were arguments not to be withstood, and away went squaws, boys, and girls, and in half an hour horses were galloped into the camp in excess of our wants.

Louis brightened up and worked with a will; all smiled and flattered, and one and another said, "*My hos you*." How vividly the words of Solomon came to our memory, "Every one is a friend to him that giveth gifts"!

The animals were soon laden; a horse was provided for the poor sufferer, William, and all things were ready for a last trip to the waters of Magellan.

We bade the Indians and the camp farewell,

and with no little emotion we said good-by to the old chief and his wife, whose kindness and sympathy we had enjoyed during our whole stay in Patagonia. On waving a final adieu to the aged couple, the old mother set up a mournful wailing in such plaintive strains as to touch our hearts. This she kept up until her form faded from our sight and the lament died upon our ears. We shall never forget the picture of sorrow presented by this mourning pair as we turned our backs upon them. We left no truer friends behind us.

Louis and a few other Indians went with us to the shore. Most of the clan spent the night on the beach.

It was now near noon, and we felt anxious lest the captain, tired of waiting for us, should have gone upon his way; but when we were within about six miles of the shore we were surprised to meet Joseph Nash, the captain's brother and the first mate of the Antarctic, and Charles Palmer, who came out with us on the Mary Jane. Mr. Nash informed us that the captain had waited anxiously for us, and fearing that we were in trouble through the treachery of the savages he had sent them to reconnoitre; that Queen Maria and several other Indians were then on board the Antarctic, and that, as the captain and officers believed a plot was laid by the Indians on shore to prevent us from getting off, Maria and her attendants would be detained on board as hostages until we and our effects were safely shipped.

Furthermore, he requested us to deploy to the right and strike the beach some half a mile from the camp; meanwhile a man at the mast-head would watch for our arrival, and at a signal he would despatch a swift boat for us, while at the same time he would send another direct to the Indian camp as a decoy; that the boat for us would strike the beach just at the time of our arrival; that we should jump aboard at once, and thus elude the Indians.

This was done with complete success, and with the skill of a military or naval tactician. The few Indians who were with us made no effort to detain us, and those at a distance made no efforts to reach us, so that their plot, if they had one, was a failure. Louis was permitted, on account of his great desire, to go on board with us.

When Captain Nash saw that we were safely embarked in the boat, he sent off another to convey Maria and her party to the shore. As this boat passed us, a savage held up a religious tract and called out to us to look on while he dashed it into the sea.

This token of contempt was at once imitated by the Queen, who raised a bundle of tracts in the air and in a spiteful manner threw them overboard, exclaiming " Malo! malo!" The captain afterwards told us that these tracts were stolen from his cabin, that Maria said we had a chest full of them, that they were very bad, and that by means of our paper we prevented them from getting rum and tobacco; that she had also complained of Mr. Arms that he was very bad, and had declared that as soon as she got on shore she would tear up the papers before his eyes, and then stab him with a knife which she drew from her bosom and showed him. These threats had led the captain to take the precaution of sending her and her people on shore while we were coming off, that thus a meeting might be avoided, as he had no doubt she would execute her threat should she find an opportunity. It might have happened so had we met the old Queen, but as we were blissfully ignorant of this danger until safe on board, we were saved from fear and anxiety. We are under great obligations to Captain Nash, who has treated us with much kindness, and who has shown firmness and discretion in getting us on board.

He told us that the old Queen showed him great ingratitude; for after supplying her and others with large quantities of bread and other eatables she told him he was "much malo" for taking us away, and that if he went on shore he would be stabbed. He tells us that our influence in endeavoring to suppress the vices of these natives is entirely counteracted by the sailors who stop here, and who tell the Indians that we came among them only to prevent them from getting such things as they want from ships; that we are bad men, and that they even advise them to destroy us. He assured us that he had men on board his own vessel who would do all this, and that one of them had been heard to tell the Indians to knock us down and throw us overboard.

We have little doubt that these are facts, as we have always found the savages worse after a visit to vessels.

Captain Nash then informed us that in coming through the Strait from the West he had spoken the Peruvian and the schooner on which I had slept about two weeks ago. The captain of that schooner had told him of my visit to his vessel, and had complained bitterly of the savages, stating that after I had left him in the morning, he sent his boat to the shore to trade, when the Indians seized the boat and his second officer, took them both up high and dry upon the banks, and then demanded a barrel of bread and five hundred plugs of tobacco as a ransom. All this he was compelled to give before he could recover his mate and boat. This, then, explains the riddle of the empty barrel on which the Indian drummed—the supply of bread shared so liberally with us, and the abundance of tobacco which we had observed at that time in the camp, and on which some of the people got deadly drunk, turning pale and groaning like dying men; for it was their custom in smoking to draw their mantles over their heads and inhale the fumes until completely intoxicated.

Captain Nash had also met the English schooner Sappho, near the western entrance of the Strait, and Captain Melward and Mr. Penny had told him of our situation, and of our desire to find a passage to the United States. Then, too, he had "gammed," or visited, on board the Mary Jane, and, by request, had taken Charles Palmer, the suffering sailor, to return him to New York.

Charles had told him much of us, and he had determined to anchor at Gregory's Bay and take us off if we were near at hand. No wonder, then, that we were surprised when he told Mr. Arms, on first meeting him, "I have come for you." In this whole chain of facts how clearly we see "the good hand of our God upon us."

There being a strong current against us and no wind, the Antarctic remained at anchor for several hours after we came on board, during which time numbers of the savages were brought off in the schooner's boats to sell guanaco robes, fresh meat, and other articles. They appeared glad to see us and behaved quietly, and when they left the vessel some inquired how soon we would return.

It is evident that most of the chiefs and the great body of the clan have no little respect for us, but they are capricious, jealous, selfish, and superstitious, so that their friendship is unreliable, and their good-will to-day may turn to anger to-morrow. One thing is clear: that their selfishness and cupidity lead them to cling to us, for they have not failed to see that we have been of service to them in many ways, and they were hoping for more help and more gifts.

Louis is on deck and keeps near us; he seems to mourn our departure, for he looks sad. And we feel sad at leaving him; for in spite of his late apparent guile, we must ever remember his great fidelity to us during our sojourn of seventy-two days in this land of darkness. Under God we look upon him as our great protector, and he seems to us as one sent of the Lord to meet and receive us on our first entrance into Patagonia, and but for his constant and watchful care we cannot now see how our lives would have been made tolerable even if spared to this day. And now as we are about to bid him a final farewell his first love seems to revive, and he clings to us like a brother and really appears anxious to go with us.

At $4\frac{1}{2}$ P.M. a light breeze began to fan the surface of the water, and the captain ordered a boat to land all the Indians that remained on board, but Louis and a few of his friends lingered. The captain called, "All hands on deck! Make sail," and, in a few minutes, "Take the anchor," but Louis still remained. The vessel was now under way and slowly moving off with the boats by her side, when the captain sternly commanded Louis and his friends to jump into the boat, which they did reluctantly. We shook hands with them and waved them adieu, and they were soon landed.

And now our prow was pointed eastward towards the great Atlantic and we were really "homeward bound." We saw the savages on the shore all astir, getting up their horses, packing, mounting, and moving off to their dismal homes. This to us was a sad picture; for though we are joyful at the thought that our exploring mission is accomplished, and that we are now on our way back to our thrice-blessed native land, and to our precious friends from whom we have received no tidings for nearly six months, yet it was painful to see these poor, dark-souled human beings for whom the Saviour died left in their darkness and ruin, and with little hope that the blessings of Christianity and civilization would ever come to their generation.

Thus commingled emotions of joy and pity move our hearts. The remembrance of their abominations pains and sickens our souls; their wretchedness excites our compassion; their kindness kindles our gratitude; and the blindness of their moral and spiritual natures awakens our sympathies and our love.

Ah! when will the day dawn and the day star arise upon them?

Well, we are in the cabin of the swift clipper Antarctic, a beautiful schooner of 173 tons, running like a racer, while the shores of Patagonia are gathering the mantle of night over them and fading from our view.

CHAPTER XII.

LIFE AT THE FALKLAND ISLANDS.

Schooner Antarctic, off Cape Virgins, Sunday, Jan. 26, 1834.—Arose this morning and found the Antarctic passing out of the Strait and driving into the billows of the Atlantic. We made a fine run during the night, and we shall soon sink all land and get an open ocean horizon.

Our young English exile is with us, very feeble, and unable to perform any labor, but exceedingly joyful in the thought that he has escaped from the grasp of the savages, and that he once more sees the faces of the civilized and the merciful. It is a comfort to see his happiness.

Charles Palmer, also, is quite jubilant in view of his situation, and his health is fast improving. In fact, it is a bright and joyful day to all on board. Even our vessel seems to leap and dance and rush into the white foam "like a thing of life."

We have a large and fine cabin, and all the appointments of this schooner are excellent, much better than those of any other sealing vessel we have seen. It is the same schooner in which Captain Benjamin Morrell once visited the South Seas and wrote the narrative that I have mentioned.

Captain Nash informs us that his ship-stores are low, and that unless he can replenish them at the Falkland Islands he will be obliged to leave us there, where there will be no difficulty in our obtaining a passage to the States.

Arrangements were made for divine service this afternoon, but before the hour arrived the sea became rough, and we were so prostrated with seasickness that the service was given up. On coming out of the Strait this morning we saw a large brig, having the appearance of a man-of-war, going in under the north shore, but so far from us the captain could not speak her.

Jan. 28. At 9 A.M. we made the Falkland Islands, and in the afternoon ran into a little bay and dropped anchor near the shore in quiet water. Here we found the schooner Caroline, Captain Storer, of New York.

As nine of our crew were going on shore to find game, and as they invited us, we went with them. The islands and lagoons of this group abound in geese, ducks, and a great variety of other fowls, and the interior in wild cattle, hogs, and rabbits.

In a short time our sailors shot thirty geese, ducks, etc., and returned on board laden with game. On returning to our vessel we found Captain Storer, of the Caroline, and Captain Benjamin Pendleton, of Stonington, Ct., master of the whaleship Hamilton, of New York, in our cabin "gamming." Captain Pendleton's ship is moored at New Island, about 70 miles from us. The Caroline is a tender for the Hamilton, and goes out into the open ocean in search of whales, and when killed tows them into the harbor, where they are "cut in" and "tried out" on board the Hamilton. These vessels have been out twelve months from the United States.

Albemarle Harbor, Falkland Islands, Jan. 29.—We are anchored in a small lagoon almost surrounded by islets. On the south is Arch Island, so named on account of a natural arch opening a passage entirely through one end of the island, so that boats and small vessels can pass in and out of the harbor under this natural bridge.

The schooner Hancock, Captain Davison, of Stonington, Ct., came into our harbor this morning. She is bound on a sealing expedition. We learn that the brig we passed in coming out of the Strait is the Beagle, Captain Fitz Roy, a surveying vessel of the British Royal Navy. (Charles Darwin was on board of her, making his famous voyage; but of that we knew nothing at the time.)

Towards evening the Antarctic left Port Albemarle, ran down the island a few miles, and anchored in a little cove. From the deck we noticed a large number of hair-seals basking in the sun on a beautiful sand-beach opposite our vessel. A boat was launched, and eighteen men, armed with guns and clubs, went on shore to attack these animals. While rowing to the shore many of the huge creatures dove into the water and came swimming around our boat, snorting, growling, and gnashing their teeth. Not to disturb those which remained on the beach, our men landed at a distance from them, and came upon them by a circuitous route; but being so near the water they killed only three, while more than a hundred escaped into the sea. One of those captured is what is called a sea-lion (*Platyrhunchus leoninus*), a name probably given him from his huge dimensions, his bold front, and his power in combat.

This animal measured ten feet and four inches in length. On being fired upon the whole drove plunged into the water, making the bay foam with their splashings. Many of them came close to the shore, grunting and growling as if to defy us. The men shot several of them in the water, but this was a pity, as it was also cruel, for they all sunk at once and could not be taken. Two large foxes, coming boldly out of the bushes to reconnoitre, were unceremoniously shot.

Bay of St. Salvador, Falkland Islands, Jan. 30. —At daylight this morning the Antarctic was got under way, and we ran down through Falkland Sound, the beautiful sheet of water which separates the two principal islands of the group, East and West Falkland, and at 4 P.M. anchored in this bay, having sailed nearly one hundred miles. Our passage through the sound was delightful. With a fine breeze and a smooth sea we glided along at the rate of ten knots an hour. The island on our left presented in many places a bold shore of perpendicular rock, while inland a range of mountains rose to a considerable height, sprinkled here and there with patches of snow. On our right the land was low and level, resembling somewhat the pampas of Eastern Patagonia. On our way through the sound we spoke two vessels. The captain's object in visiting this bay is to get some spars and other articles left here by the Antarctic on her way out, and also to make some repairs on the vessel before going to sea.

Went ashore at 5 P.M. with several of the crew in search of game. Immediately on landing we saw a sea-elephant on the beach. Coming between it and the sea, it came towards us displaying enormous open jaws and strong teeth, when our officer fired directly into its mouth—the surest way of killing the monster—and brought him down. He measured fifteen and a half feet, and he will yield about three barrels of oil. The sea-elephant (*Macrorhinus proboscidens*) is the largest species of seal. It is said to be sometimes found measuring thirty feet in length and yielding twenty-five barrels of oil. It is a formidable-looking animal, but on account of its clumsiness on land it is not at all dangerous, though powerful in the water. Having flippers instead of legs, it only moves by awkward and slow hitches on the land, so that a boy of four years can outrun it. Our men shot several geese and ducks, and we returned to the schooner.

Feb. 1. Three men appearing on horseback upon

THE FALKLAND ISLANDS.

the shore opposite our vessel, the captain sent a boat to communicate with them. The boat returned and reported that they were Mestizos and Indians from Buenos Ayres who had lived at Port Louis, and who roamed over the islands to slaughter wild cattle and other game. They are called Gauchos. Port Louis was a small Spanish settlement, and the only village on the island, Port Egmont, a small English settlement, having been abandoned. We hear that there has has been a massacre at Port Louis of late. This port was formerly under a governer named Vernit, who was commissioned by the Buenos Ayres Government, and a man of the name of Brisbane, an Englishman, acted as lieutenant-governor. This colony attempted to monopolize the seal-fishery about these islands, seizing American vessels, confiscating their cargoes, and putting their crews into confinement, or banishing them to other islands.

In 1831 the United States sloop-of-war Lexington was sent out to break up the establishment. Governor Vernit fled to Buenos Ayres, Brisbane was taken prisoner and sent to the same place, and the nest was broken up.

After this the English took possession of the

islands, and a small colony was begun at Port Louis, to which Brisbane returned as acting-governor. Displeasing the few Spaniards, mestizos and Indians of the place, they arose, and on the 26th of August, 1833, murdered Brisbane and four others of the colonists, intending, obviously, to massacre the whole English colony. In this they failed, as the rest of the residents rushed into a stone house with a few arms, barricaded it, and determined to sell their lives, if need be, at the highest cost. The murderers watched the house for a day or two, and finding it too dangerous to storm, they tore down the other houses of the village, broke up all the boats or sent them adrift, sacked the village, drove off all the domestic animals—horses, sheep, swine, horned cattle, etc.—and decamped to a sheltered valley on the other side of the island. After the murderers had left the place the barricaded men came out, and looked for some way of escape from the island.

Fortunately one of the boats which the mob had set adrift upon the water floated across the channel and beached on the opposite shore. One of the men, being a good swimmer, succeeded in reaching it, got it afloat, and sculled it across the channel to his companions, who all embarked immediately and escaped to another island, where they awaited a vessel which relieved them. In due time the news of the massacre was sent to the British naval commander at Buenos Ayres, when a lieutenant of the Royal Navy with six marines was sent to Port Louis to hold the place until sufficient help should be sent.

This we understand to be the present state of things at the islands, and the three men seen on the shore to-day, armed to the teeth, are probably of the murderous gang from Port Louis. They inquired if our vessel wanted fresh beef and promised us a fat cow this afternoon if the captain would send his boat some four or five miles down the coast to a lagoon where they would deliver it. They also agreed to deliver the captain seven fat bullocks to-morrow at five dollars a head, taking pay in powder, balls, tobacco, rum, and other articles.

A boat was sent for the beef promised to-day, and Mr. Arms and I went in it. The sailors had a long and hard pull, and only reached the cove a little before sundown. Here in a most secluded nook, covered by hills and open only to the sea, we found seven armed men, Spaniards and Indians, dressing a fat cow. They looked wild and suspicious, and we supposed them to have been engaged in the massacre of last August. Our men took the beef, and we returned to the Antarctic, arriving at 10 P.M.

Feb. 3. At an early hour this morning six men appeared on the shore with eleven horses and four beeves. The bullocks were purchased for our vessel, and a bright, active little Spaniard with one attendant came on board to receive the pay. These men are armed with double-barrelled guns, pistols, dirks, and knives. The Spaniard is the evident leader of the gang, and they call him Captain Antook. Having received the pay for the animals, he bowed a polite good-day and was off in trice. His eye was sharp and restless, and his bearing like that of one ill at ease.

Feb. 4. We saw two men on the beach this morning, and a boat was sent to speak them. They proved to be an Englishman and an Indian from Port Louis, on the opposite side of this island, and were supposed to have been sent by Lieutenant Smith to inquire about our vessel.

In the afternoon they came down again, and the Englishman came on board with a letter from the Governor to Captain Nash. This letter gave many particulars in regard to the bloody massacre at the Port, stating also that the Indian who accompanies the Englishman was one of the murderers who had given himself up to the Governor, and received pardon on promising to become a witness for the Crown.

This Indian brought back two horses, and these are all that can be mustered at Port Louis, the gauchos having taken off fifty when they left the place.

Feb. 5. Governor Smith came over from Port Louis to-day, accompanied by Captain Rea, six English marines, and the Indian who gave himself up. Captain Rea is in the service of the English Admiralty, and in attempting to reach the newly discovered "Graham's Land" lost his vessel, but succeeded in reaching the Falkland Islands with his secretary, Mr. Foxton, where they are now waiting for a chance to return to England.

Coming on board the Antarctic, the Governor and the captain began a conversation with Captain Nash about the massacre. Having heard that Captain Nash had aided and abetted these desperadoes, the Governor's language waxed warm and threatening. He even declared that if he had an armed vessel he would proceed immediately to seize the Antarctic. He blamed Captain Nash severely for trading with these ruffians and receiving them on board his vessel, styling it an act of hostility against "His Majesty's Government," and especially blaming him for not arresting the murderers when they came on board. The Governor affirmed that Captain Nash had involved himself and his country in serious difficulty with the Government of Great Britain. Captain Nash replied that he had been greatly misinformed: that only one of the company, An-took, with an attendant, had been on board the Antarctic, and that this was at a time when two of his sailors were on shore and in the power of the rest of the gang of supposed murderers. Besides, he asserted that he had no evidence but that of suspicion and rumor that the men with whom he traded were the party guilty of the massacre; that he had no legal warrant from any source to seize them; and finally, that, had he arrested them, he then had no authentic information of the reëstablishment of any government on the islands, civil, military, or naval, to which he could deliver them. On these grounds he felt himself clear from all complicity with the crimes alleged, and from all blame in the offences charged upon him.

In reply to the threatenings of the Governor, Captain Nash stated that he had a good vessel armed with six brass nine-pounders, with plenty of powder and balls, also a full complement of muskets, pistols, cutlasses, harpoons, spades, and boarding pikes, and that he was well able to defend himself, but that notwithstanding this, since the Governor was without an " armed vessel," he would consent to take the Antarctic to Port Louis and deliver her up to him if he desired it.

The atmosphere of the cabin now became cooler; the Governor began to retract, saying, " No, no, I do not wish it," and after fuller explanations he became very pacific and courteous. All matters of difference were amicably settled, and the Governor cordially invited Captain Nash to visit Port Louis in the Antarctic, offering him any assistance in his power.

The Governor and Captain Rea then held a pleasant conversation with Mr. Arms and myself, and the Governor insisted on our going home with him to spend the night, offering to give us fresh milk and butter and the best of all he had, and then to send his marines to escort us back to the schooner on the morrow.

We accepted the invitation with pleasure, and at 4 P.M. set off for the Port, where we arrived at a quarter past eight, distance ten or twelve miles. There were but two horses in the party of eleven. One of these the pardoned Indian was permitted to ride as his own, while the other was appropriated to Captain Rea, my companion, and myself, by order of the Governor, who with his marines insisted on walking all the way. We had no road or trail, but took the direction towards Port Louis, passing over fields of grass, sometimes thick and tall like tussock-grass (Dactylis), and sometimes over low grassy plains. Where the tall or bunch grasses were abundant the rabbits were very numerous, and our company caught a full dozen on the way. These were found with great ease, simply by watching for the animals as they ran for shelter into thick tufts of grass.

The tussock has a succulent and nutritious root on which the rabbit, the wild hog, the rat, and other rodents feed.

Port Louis consists of a dozen low houses, some built of stone and others of turf or *adobe*, and all thatched with grass. As before stated, most of these houses were pulled down or unroofed by the gauchos, so that when Lieut. Smith came with his six marines to act as Governor of the islands, he had first to roof a part of a stone house to obtain comfortable shelter.

Into this house of one room we were kindly and courteously welcomed, and here with the Governor, Captain Rea, and Mr. Foxton we spent a pleasant night.

One or two other houses have been partially repaired, furnishing rude quarters for the marines and a few sailors, adventurers, etc., amounting in all to twenty-three men.

The Governor's quarters contained one old Franklin stove, a table, an old sideboard, a dingy sofa, a chest of drawers, a crib, and a few chairs.

In this room Governor Brisbane was murdered, and here we heard an account of the shocking event and its immediate cause.

Brisbane employed the Spaniard Antook as a shoemaker, and several Mestizos and South American Indians as herdsmen, bullock-hunters, etc. Failing to pay them promptly, from lack of means, as he said, they were angry, and determined to kill him and all his friends and plunder the village. According to the plot agreed on, Antook came to the door of this room one morning while Brisbane was sitting before the stove lighted with a fire of peat, the principal fuel of these islands, and demanded pay. Brisbane refused, and immediately a bullet went through his body.

He grabbed for his pistol, in a cupboard on his left, arose to fire, but staggered and fell, when he received a blow upon his head from a cutlass and three stabs from a dirk. He was then dragged to the door, his feet bound with raw-hide rope, and this being attached to the saddle of a horse, he was drawn out into the field, where he was stripped, mutilated, and left unburied. His clerk was also killed with several others at the same time, and the town was sacked, a few Englishmen escaping as before stated.

Governor Smith had succeeded in catching two wild milch-cows, and he redeemed his hospitable word by giving us fresh milk and butter, with eggs, fresh beef, sea-biscuit, etc., making a delicious supper.

The evening passed pleasantly in talk with the Governor and Captain Rea on their expeditions, perils, and varied experiences in the wild regions of the Antarctic Ocean. The hour of sleep arriving, Mr. Arms and myself were furnished with a narrow crib bed and a sofa, while the other three were disposed, one on the broad window-sill, one on the table, and the other on the floor, and thus we passed the night, the marines standing their appointed watches until morning.

Feb. 6. At a little before 11 A.M. we left Port Louis and set out for Salvador Bay. We declined an escort of marines, very kindly offered by the Governor, telling him we only needed the old Gaucho to guide us. The Governor gave us the spare horse and a sailor to go with us and bring him back. In order to quicken our speed, we doubled the horses, the sailor riding behind the Indian, and Mr. Arms and I occupying the other saddle. But we worked our passages, for propelling the old worn-out horse was like setting an old leaky scow up stream. However, we arrived at the bay in good time, and were taken on board the Antarctic.

Feb. 8. Our anchor was taken up this morning and our sails spread for a visit to Eagle Island; but as the wind failed, the tide drifted the Antarctic towards the shore and she grounded. A kedge anchor was carried out from her bows, and she was soon hauled off into deep water. A breeze now sprung up and we beat out of the bay.

Learning that a French man-of-war and an

English schooner had just arrived at Port Louis, our captain determined to pass that way and send a boat from the mouth of Berkley Sound, sixteen miles, to Port Louis, to ascertain what ship it was, and to get some small stores, if possible, for our vessel.

Feb. 9. Calm all the afternoon of yesterday and all last night. This morning we found our vessel drifted quite into the entrance of Berkley Sound, where we saw the French ship beating out against a head-wind. As she passed near us our captain spoke her, and found her to be the Victorious, twenty-two days from Rio and bound to Valparaiso.

Our boat returned at 10½ A.M. with an earnest request from Governor Smith for the Antarctic to visit Port Louis, and we immediately squared away and ran before the wind to the Port, and at 2 P.M. came to anchor in the harbor. Here we found the English schooner Hopeful, Captain Mallros, who with another gentleman came at once on board our vessel.

Feb. 11. Took a ramble on shore this morning to see the village cemetery. This, like the village and all its surroundings, is in a neglected and dilapidated condition. Four rude **boards** mark the resting-places of as many English and American seamen. All the other graves are undistinguished by any memorial of their tenants. We visited the great *corral*, or cattle-pen, in which a hundred horned cattle were sometimes collected for slaughter or for taming. Only eleven bullocks are now in this enclosure; for although there are numerous wild cattle on the group, yet for lack of horses and expert lasso-men but few have been taken since the massacre.

We called on the Governor and took a walk with him in his garden and in the fields. The former contains an acre of ground, but he arrived too late in the season to cultivate many vegetables this year. The soil is good, but the warm season is short in this high latitude. Irish potatoes, beans, turnips, and some other vegetables of quick growth can be raised here.

One of our boats went out on a fishing expedition to-day, and returned loaded with fishes as large as shad and greater in number than the surprising draught of Peter. The coves and lagoons of these islands are well stocked with fishes, which can be easily taken in a net in large quantities.

Choiseul Bay, Feb. 12.—We left Port Louis this morning for Eagle Island. While getting under way the Governor came on board to bring some despatches and to bid us farewell. Captain Mallros, of the Hopeful, also paid us a pleasant visit, sailing some distance down the sound with us, and then returning in his boat to his vessel.

Captain Prior, of the English sloop which was lost in the ice off the Southern Ocean, takes passage for himself and four of his crew for New Island on board the Antarctic.

While passing the South Rocks in the mouth of Berkley Sound we saw them covered with furseals, while the waters around the rocks were alive with the gambols of these animals. We supposed that there were at least a thousand of them.

Clark's Harbor, Eagle Island, Feb. 14.—In consequence of calms we reached this port only this morning. Most of the crew have spent the day on shore in search of wild hogs and other game. Several geese and a variety of birds were taken, but no hogs.

Feb. 15. Went on shore in company with a boat's crew in search of wild geese. Twelve were shot, together with many smaller fowls and a beautiful white swan. Just at night two schooners came into the harbor and anchored near us:

the Unicorn, an armed English vessel engaged in surveying these islands, and the Elizabeth Jane, Captain Alberton, of New York. Captain Alberton came on board our vessel.

Sunday, Feb. 16.—Captain Nash invited the masters, officers, and crews of the two schooners to attend divine service on board the Antarctic. At the hour appointed a signal was set, and these hardy sons of the ocean collected together and filled our cabin. It was a pleasure to meet so large a number of the human brotherhood on these lonely isles in the far south. Here the Englishman, the Frenchman, American, Scotchman, Irishman, German, and African met to recognize the one fatherhood of God, the one brotherhood of man, the one blood of all nations, the one Lord's day for all Christians, the one Bible as the light of the earth, and the one Saviour of a lost world. What ties can so truly bind the human family together as these?

Feb. 18. After beating all day against a head-wind in company with the Elizabeth Jane, we were unable yesterday to reach the place of our destination, Arch Island, and so came to anchor at night under lee of the shore. Early this morning we entered Port Albemarle. Here we found the ship Charles Adams, Captain Staunton, of Stonington, Ct., with her tender, the brig Uxor; also the bark Commodore Barre, Captain Chester, of New York. These vessels are all engaged in whaling. There are now five sail lying in the port, giving it a lively appearance.

The safe and quiet harbors of this group are numerous, and many of them are landlocked. Many ships, barks, brigs, and schooners flock together in these bays.

Captain Nash tells us to-day that, not being able to obtain suitable provisions here, he will be obliged to leave us with some of the vessels at these islands, whence we will, as he thinks, soon find passage to the United States. He now purposes to visit St. Charles, in Brazil, for supplies and repairs. So our hopes of a speedy return to our country are again disappointed. But all will be right, and in God's good time we hope to see the land of our birth.

Fish Bay, Feb. 19.—Left Port Albemarle for New Island. We passed many islands of various forms and sizes, some of which were crowded with birds, which filled the air with wild and various notes. We estimated that twenty thousand birds were sometimes seen on an islet of two miles in circumference. There is a gregarious bird very common here which the sailors call "Johnny Rook." This rook (*Corvus frugilegus*) resembles the crow. Some of its habits are amusing, though often vexatious. He is an arrant rogue, and outdoes all the feathered tribe in impudence. Johnny is always watching the sailor when on shore, hovering and screaming just over his head, following him from place to place, and when he lays any small article upon the ground, slyly stealing it away, often from within two feet of him. He seems to delight in mischief for its own sake. He has often been known to break large quantities of eggs which sailors had gathered and left only for a few minutes unguarded. This is done wantonly, and not from hunger. He will even watch when any one buries a small article in the ground, and will dig it up and, if possible, destroy it, or carry it away and hide it. He has been known to take pocket-knives, powder-horns, flasks, caps, handkerchiefs, etc., and sometimes to drop them into the middle of a pond in sight of their owners. These vexatious habits render the rook an object of resentment to the sailors, and, as the bird is easily captured, the most shocking tortures are often inflicted upon it.

Feb. 20. Captain Nash has concluded to remain in this harbor until he leaves the islands. He therefore sent a boat to New Island—seven miles—to communicate with some ships lying there and with Captain Benjamin Pendleton, of the ship Hamilton.

Wishing to find a home for my companion and myself when the Antarctic shall leave us, I took passage in the boat this morning for Island Harbor. The day was very stormy and cold, but we reached the Hamilton in good time, and were kindly received by Captain Pendleton and invited to spend the night on board, which invitation was thankfully accepted. This is a fine ship of 500 tons, with two schooners attached as tenders. Captain Pendleton very generously offers us a home on board his vessel until we find an opportunity to sail for the States. Here I found some trunks and other articles we left on board the Mary Jane to be sent back to the United States.

I also found two young sailors who escaped from Patagonia in the Macdonough two days before we embarked in the antarctic.

Feb. 21. We received an invitation to return to Fish Bay in the schooner Hancock, Captain Davison. In two hours we were alongside of the Antarctic.

Feb. 23. Yesterday was mostly spent by the crew in getting ready for sea, and by us in preparing letters, etc., for our friends, if this vessel should chance to reach home before us.

Feb. 24. We bade farewell to the Antarctic to-day, and took up our lodgings on board the Hamilton.

Captain Nash refuses to take any compensation for our board and passage. We have been with him a full month, and we feel under great obligations for the generous welcome he has given us and for all that we have enjoyed in his beautiful and comfortable vessel, in which we have been conveyed from port to port, until we have seen most that is to be seen among these islands.

Feb. 26. The Antarctic sailed this morning with fair weather and a brisk breeze, and was soon out of sight.

Captain Pendleton tells us to make ourselves quite at home, and gives us evidence of a sincere welcome. Two boats went out in search of whales. A large whale was harpooned, but as the sea was rough the line was cut in order to save the boat and the lives of the crew: so the monster made off with the barbed iron in his flesh.

Captain Davison, of the Hancock, came on board and told us that the schooner Talma, Captain Gordon Allyn, of New London, was daily expected in from the South Shetland Islands, and that he was quite sure he could procure for us a passage in her. He added that he was bound to a certain harbor where he expected to meet the Talma, as she was mated with the Hancock in the seal-fishery. He then invited one or both of us to come on board his vessel and make it our home, while he waited and watched for the Talma. It was soon arranged that I should go with Captain Davison, while Mr. Arms would remain on the Hamilton ready to sail for home should the opportunity present. The Hamilton immediately sailed down to West Point Harbor, a distance of thirty miles. Here we anchored for the purpose of taking fish and fowl.

Ship Harbor, Feb. 28. Spent the last two days chiefly in reading, in conversation with the captain and officers, etc., and in rambling on shore.

There is little variety in the scenery of these islands. Barren rocks, heath-clad hills, swales of coarse, rank grass, with here and there an island of peat and tussock, are the chief objects of an inanimate kind which meet the eye; while the ear is constantly saluted with the harsh croaking of unnumbered sea-fowls and the ceaseless roar of the surges as they dash among the craggy cliffs of an iron-bound shore.

March 1. Took a ramble this morning upon this desolate island, and here in this dreary solitude I found a little nameless cemetery where the remains of seven sailors' sleep alone. The sight awakened sad reflections.

Sunday, March 2. The morning opened with great beauty and sweet serenity.

Captain Davison is very kind and affable, and not averse to conversation on the most important of all themes which concern man. He seems candid and thoughtful, and his conduct is very courteous.

Arrangements were made by him for religious service in the afternoon, but just before the hour arrived the cry of " Sail ho!" rang from the deck. A schooner was descried coming rapidly into the harbor, and it was soon found to be the Talma, bound for New London! In she came and dropped anchor near the Hancock, and the "gamming" commenced immediately. There was general joy in meeting old friends and neighbors, and of telling the "yarns" of the sea. I was introduced to Captain Allyn, and when Captain Davison told him our Patagonian history and our desire to return to the United States, he at once offered us a passage, though he has a large crew and little provision. The fact that he intends to sail as soon as possible is cheering, after the delays and uncertainties of the past weeks.

March 5. We left Ship Harbor in the Hancock yesterday to return to the Hamilton. On account of a calm we made little progress all day and all the night, but at seven this morning we anchored near the Hamilton, and found one of her tenders "cutting in" what they called a hundred-barrel whale, while the whole train of large pots on deck were smoking with the boiling blubber. Captain Allyn remained at Ship Harbor to prepare for his voyage north, promising to come for us at New Island when he shall be ready for sea. We are under great obligations to Captain Davison for his prompt, kind, and courteous agency in securing us a passage in the Talma, to which he would convey us with our effects, even though ready to sail as soon as the wind shall favor, for the Strait of Magellan, could he obtain the consent of his crew.

March 6. A bright morning, with a crisp northerly wind. Shortly after the departure of the Hancock, the whaleship Atlantic, of Bridgeport, Conn., Captain Young, came into this harbor, which is to be his place of rendezvous. These whalers have many a sad tale of danger and disaster to tell. Captain Young has lost one man on his way out. Two of his boats were in pursuit of a large whale. One boat-steerer struck the whale with his harpoon and "made fast." The furious monster turned directly upon the boat, struck it a full blow with his fluke, cut it in two, shivered it, killed one man instantly, and scattered the rest of the boat's crew upon the water, where they would all have perished had it not been for the proximity of a second boat in which they were taken and saved. It is an important precaution observed by whalemen to send out their boats in pairs.

One of the Hamilton's boats fastened to a huge whale, but he towed the boat so swiftly through the water that the raw sailors took fright and leaped overboard, choosing rather to wait for a slower boat than to take passage in one that turned the blue into white, and seemed to them to outstrip the wind. The consequence of this plunge was that the boat-steerer was obliged to cut the line, stop the mad rush of the boat, pick up his men, and lose the whale.

At 4 P.M. to-day the Talma came in and anchored near the Hamilton. Captain Allyn has been faithful to his promise to come for us. Had it not been to accommodate us, he would have taken his departure for the United States directly from Ship Harbor. Thus all things work favorably for us, and we have abundant reason to be thankful. There are two ships and four schooners in this harbor to-day, and all the masters are from the little busy beehive State of Connecticut. There is much of "gamming," or visiting from vessel to vessel, except when whales are being taken. Then all hands are astir, and there is little rest by day or by night.

March 8. Went on shore with a guide this morning to take my last ramble upon these islands. After walking over a steep hill and through rank tussock-grass for a mile and a half, we came to a large rookery of penguins, albatrosses, mollemokes (*Procellaria glacialis*), and other birds.

This rookery covers several acres, and we are

told that in the season of incubation it is so completely filled with birds that the ground can hardly be seen, and eggs can be gathered by thousands on thousands. Most of these birds have reared their young and left the rookery, but several thousands still remain, as their broods are not old enough to leave their nests.

When the penguins are sufficiently grown they are led like soldiers in single file to the shore, when they take to the sea and are seen no more until the time for laying returns. They are amphibious, seeming to be half fish, half fowl. They are web-footed, with feathers resembling large and coarse scales, and with only the stumps of wings.

They walk erect, but cannot fly. In the water they use both their stumps of wings and their webbed feet, and are expert swimmers and divers. They are often seen hundreds of miles from land, where they are perfectly at home in storm or calm.

In the rookery we saw several nests of the albatross. These were built of mud, grass, small stones, and sticks, say two feet high, and as large as a barrel. These nests overlook the rookery, and they seem to stand as so many round towers for the posting of sentinels. The penguins and other fowls lay on the ground, making only a slight depression in the earth for a nest.

I found some of the nests with the young albatross on, about two thirds grown, or the size of a goose. These were not sufficiently fledged to fly, but kept to their towers day and night, too large to be brooded, but still receiving their daily food from the parent-birds. I saw but one bird in a nest, and inferred that the albatross lays but one egg in a season. On approaching one of these cumbrous young birds it seemed much disturbed, hissed angrily, and showed fight.

In the afternoon we took all our baggage on board the Talma, as the captain declares himself ready to sail to-morrow. Captain Pendleton not only refuses all remuneration for our board while with him, but he is also determined to supply us with "small stores" and other provisions for the voyage home. Captain Young, of the Atlantic, also begs the privilege to join in this generous work, while the masters of the schooners wish to have a hand in seeing us well supplied. Everywhere the true sailor is proverbial for his generosity, and everywhere we have experienced only kindness from our brethren of the sea and of the land.

We have now been at these islands forty days save one, and expect to leave on the fortieth. We have met hundreds of our fellow-men of about twelve different nationalities. We have received nothing but respect and kindness from all; and we have endeavored so to live among them as to convince all of our earnest desire for their welfare here and forever.

CHAPTER XIII.

HOMEWARD BOUND.

Schooner Talma, at Sea, March 9, 1834.—The morning opened with golden light, the sky was clear, the wind fair, and we got under way at an early hour. With her prow to the north our sea-gull schooner danced along her track, gliding rapidly over the waters like a bird just set free from its cage and rejoicing to spread its pinions to the morning breeze. The weather continued fine during the day, and the shores and lowlands of the islands sunk below our horizon; then the table-lands disappeared, and before dark the higher and then the highest points of the land (fifteen hundred feet in elevation) were submerged beneath the waves.

March 15. For three days past we have been among ice-bergs, some of them several miles in length and perhaps a hundred feet high. The chill of these monstrous congelations strikes us strongly. Our captain navigates carefully while in near proximity to them, but our vessel is small and in such constant and violent agitation from the waves that I can do little else than brace myself and hold on.

March 23. The weather has been fine for many days, and we have held divine service on board for two Sundays, with full attendance and attention.

April 1—lat. 13° S. We passed several vessels, and before noon we made land on the coast of Brazil, distant thirty miles. As we drew nearer and nearer the shore we could see the houses on the beach and the trees along the coast.

April 5. We have now been running for five days along the shores of Brazil. The sea is smooth, the winds gentle, and the sailing delightful. The weather is warm, the mercury standing at 80° Fahr. We keep so near the shore in the daytime that we not only see the villages as we glide along, but also men on the beach and the small boats in shore.

We have passed among many catamarans, a clumsy kind of raft, or float, made of three or four logs hewed underneath at the prow, and lashed firmly together and rigged with mast, sail, and a centre-board, with a raised platform over a portion of the raft on which the fishermen sit with their tackle and bait, just above the water. On this rude float they often venture far out to sea without fear of upsetting, and not minding the wetting which is a matter of course.

As we sail smoothly along, our sailors throw out hook and line over the stern and often haul in the fine *bonito* (*Thynnus pelamys*) and other edible fishes, so that our table is well supplied. We can also purchase fish from the catamarans at almost any time.

The shores by which we pass are sometimes bold, but in most places they are low and bordered by a beautiful sand-beach, while all the back country, so far as we can see, appears beautifully tropical.

April 6. This morning we descried the city of Pernambuco, or Recife, and, being becalmed, the captain determined to go on shore and procure fruits and vegetables. He left the vessel at 9½ A. M. and returned at 5 P. M., bringing a large quantity of oranges and fresh vegetables.

During this time the Talma was lying off and on in full view of the city, and on her inland tack running close up to the harbor. The city is said to contain 30,000 inhabitants, mostly Portuguese and slaves. It is built upon low ground, and is separated into three parts by the windings of a small river. The houses are mostly built of brick and stone, with roofs of tile and grated rather than glazed windows. The buildings are generally whitewashed, which gives the city a beautiful appearance at a little distance. But it is said that much of the beauty is lost on a near view. The streets are narrow, irregular, and dirty; the front of the town extends about a mile on the shore, and many of the mercantile houses are built on spiles and stand over the water.

The harbor is narrow and extends the whole length of the town in front. It is formed by a remarkable natural wall or breakwater of rocks running parallel with the shore, and protecting it from the heavy swell of the Atlantic. The entrance of the harbor is on the north end of the town, and this pass is guarded by several forts. Here a boat is always in waiting to hail everything which attempts to enter the port, and the smallest boat is not permitted to land until it has been boarded and inspected by an officer. We are told that the smallest craft, even to a skiff, is not permitted to land until eighteen dollars are paid as port charges. This was hard on our captain, who only wished to purchase a little fruit, etc.

Two and a half miles to the north of Pernambuco stands the village of Olinda, situated upon the sides and summit of a beautifully rounded hill. This village is open, airy, and pleasant. The houses are white, and are among lovely gardens and luxuriant groves of tropical trees and shrubbery.

As seen from the sea this village presents a scene of almost unrivalled loveliness; but it might lose, like Pernambuco, some of its charms upon a nearer view.

A smooth sand-beach extends all the way from Pernambuco to Olinda. To the south of the city lies Cocoanut Island, covered all over with the cocoa-palm, whose tufted tops meet and interlock, forming a beautiful canopy of perennial green. The island is low and level, and at a little distance it presents the appearance of a floating garden. In the rear of the city the land is low and covered with trees and verdure, and the whole scene terminates in a mountain ridge of moderate elevation.

A whaling brig from the African coast, belonging to New Bedford, has lately been seized here by the U. S. consul, Mr. Halsey, and the crew are now lodged in prison on the charge of mutiny and murder. It is supposed that the master, mate, steward, and cook are all murdered, as they are missing.

We leave the coast of Brazil to-night, having been in near view of it for nearly six days, and having sailed along its tropical shores for more than three hundred English miles.

Sunday, April 20—lat. 12° N. We have left the Southern Hemisphere behind us, and are making good progress towards our northern homes.

The weather being fine, we had religious worship on deck conducted by Mr. Arms. Some of the crew seemed sober-minded; but one of the customs of the vessel has an unhappy influence upon the minds of the sailors. It is the practice of giving to every man who will take it a glass of rum on Saturday evening.

The effect is often ludicrous and yet painful. In a few minutes after swallowing the potation the men become noisy and garrulous. Some begin to harangue the rest; some tell stories; some wrestle; some sing songs; others dance with such fury as almost to blister their bare feet, and all seem to strive to perform the most comical feats possible, extorting smiles even from a weeper, and tears from a laugher. In this way most of the Saturday evenings are spent, and the carousal often runs into the night; and without great vigilance on the part of the master and officers it would often end in fighting and bloodshed.

At the best it is demoralizing, and it is an unhappy preparation for Sunday. A few of the sailors refuse to drink, and the captain seldom uses intoxicants. He talks rationally on the subject of abstinence, and says he thinks seriously of joining the temperance ranks. Some of the men who forget themselves in the "spree" seem to be ashamed of it the next day.

April 26. Made a few remarks to Mr.—— on the subject of religion. He seemed disposed to converse, and said that he had wished for an opportunity to tell me something of his history. We agreed to set apart an hour in the evening for this purpose.

At the hour appointed we met, and he related the following facts in regard to himself:

"Six years ago," he said, "I enlisted in the United States army and was stationed at one of the posts on the lines. Many of my officers were pious, and we had worship in the garrison on the Sabbath. A young clergyman frequently preached to us in the fort, and I becamed aroused to seek the salvation of my soul. I thought I found

Christ: I united with the church, joined the temperance society, and for a season sincerely felt that I enjoyed the love of God. But the tempter came. A young woman was living in the garrison who attracted my attention and won my heart. I resolved to marry her; but knowing that my officers would disapprove of such a step, I managed to have the union solemnized without their knowledge. It was, however, soon discovered, and I was put in confinement for two days.

"My wife was not pious, and I soon found that she was intemperate. I expostulated with her in her sober moments and she promised to reform, but instead of this she grew worse and worse, and in her fits of intoxication she would attack me with abusive language, and often in the presence of others, so that I was ashamed and grieved and knew not what to do.

"At length my term of service in the army expired, and I resolved to leave her and return to my friends in Maryland. This I did, but I threw off my Christian character and have never been known since as a professor of religion. My troubles preyed upon my spirits and I had no rest. I went to New York and shipped for a voyage at sea; but since I left home my bosom has been full of trouble and conflict like the restless element on which I am tossed. I am sometimes almost driven to distraction and desperation. I have given up all Christian duties and indulged in many vices, supposing that I had committed the unpardonable sin and that further efforts for salvation were fruitless. But while you were preaching the other Sabbath I felt my heart kindle with a desire to return if there be yet any hope in my case, and I wished to have this conversation with you to know what you think of me, and whether there is any hope for me."

My heart was melted with this sad story. I endeavored to point out the Scripture evidences of discipleship, viz., loving obedience to the commands of Christ, telling him that his conversion appeared like that of a "stony-ground" hearer, warning him to place no reliance at all on any former experience, and at the same time exhorting him not to despair of mercy through Christ Jesus. I told him there was one and only one safe way for him, and that was to come with "a broken and contrite heart" and throw himself at the feet of Jesus, with an honest and fixed resolution to "go and sin no more." This he promised to do, and to repair, as far as was in his power, the evils he had done, and also to return immediately to his wife on his arrival in our country.

Sunday, May 4. I talked this morning with a young man on the subject of the soul's salvation. He was a moral man, had a pleasant young wife and two children, and was engaged in a lucrative business in one of our cities. In an evil hour he was persuaded to drink to excess, and while in this state he was urged to ship on a sealing voyage to the Antarctic regions, and was hurried off by those whose "tender mercies are cruel." When he became sober he saw the rash step he had taken, and would have turned back, but it was too late. For nearly two years he has looked back with yearning desires to his injured wife and deserted babes, mourning over his folly, and longing to return to his once happy condition in the bosom of domestic love. He has resolved never more to taste the poison which deceived and maddened him, and to live a virtuous life, endeavoring to atone for his past delinquencies. Seeming not to realize that his sins were against *God*, I endeavored to fix his attention on that vital point, apprising him of the danger of trusting to the resolutions of an unchanged and unsanctified heart to keep him in the path of virtue, and urging the duty and importance of "repentance toward God and faith in the Lord Jesus Christ." He listened attentively, and evidently with tender feelings, promising to attend to the counsels given him. But ah! the sad history of the sailor! The story of one is but the story of thousands. How impressive the declaration of an ancient prophet, and how appropriate: "There is sorrow on the sea"! I preached in the afternoon from Eccl. viii. 11. We daily pass many vessels, and are looking out for land.

Monday, May 5. Saw schooners lying to and fishing for mackerel. Spoke a schooner bound to Philadelphia. The captain tells us that we are only forty-one miles from Block Island.

At 3 P.M. the cry "Land ho! land ho!" rang through our vessel. Every face brightened at the sight of our native shores, and every heart seemed to beat faster with the hope of treading the soil of New England before we slept.

As we drew near the land, it proved to be the south side of Long Island, about 20 miles west of Montauk Point. To round the cape we had to beat against a strong head-wind, which by 6 P.M. increased to a gale. The struggle to get around the eastern point of the island was earnest and hard, but unsuccessful; so at twilight the command came from the quarter deck, "Keep her off." This implied standing out to sea for the night. It was hard but necessary. The thrill of joy which went through our hearts at the thought of being in New London harbor to-night was all changed to disappointment. So we went about and ran back to the south before a gale, and meantime the rain fell in torrents. When the Talma was far enough at sea to be out of danger of the land she was hove to and suffered to drift.

We have had no gale equal to this since we left the Falkland Islands, and 'this hindrance teaches us that "our times are in His hands" who "rules the raging of the sea."

May 6. The storm abated this morning, but we had drifted out of sight of land, and it was sunset before we came up again to Montauk Point.

So we retire to rest not expecting to reach New London to-night.

New London Harbor, May 7. At 1 o'clock, A.M., while lying in our berths, we heard the plunge of the anchor, and the announcement from the deck, "All safe in New London Harbor!"

When daylight appeared our vessel was thronged with citizens who came on board to meet their friends and to inquire about the voyage.

The scene on board and on shore was very touching. Here were husbands, fathers, sons, and brothers inquiring after dear ones left behind two years ago, and from whom nothing had been heard during this long period. One of the officers was told that his only son, on whom he doted, was dead.

Another was weeping at the tidings of a fond mother and sister gone forever from earth.

But the saddest case of all was that of the young husband and father with whom I conversed last Sunday. He was met with the report that after his departure his wife came to New London in search of him, and on learning that he had sailed, she, with a broken heart, took her two children and returned to some friends in New York, where she soon sickened and died of the cholera; that one of her little ones soon followed her to the grave, leaving only one poor solitary child to meet the father. I saw the man crushed under a weight of woe which no human power could remove. It seemed as if the life would go out of him, for he had so longed to return to his injured wife and forsaken children, to confess his folly like the prodigal. And he had so reformed his habits, and so carefully husbanded his earnings at sea to cheer and comfort his family, that the disappointment was anguish.

In this state I left him with a sense of utter inability to help. Thanks be to God, there is no human sorrow so heavy that it cannot be removed by the Great Physician.

We bade our captain, officers, and sailors an affectionate farewell, and accepted the invitation of Major Williams as his guests while in the city.

Major Williams is one of the owners of the Talma, and in consultation with his partner we were informed that our passage from the Falkland Islands to New London was free.

Thus from our embarkation in New York for Patagonia until we landed on the shores of the Connecticut, we have not been called to spend one dollar of the money of the American Board. All has been free on the part of ship owners and masters, and we have been most kindly guided, protected, and blessed by Him that "keepeth Israel," and who has said, "Lo! I am with you alway."

Boston, May 8, 1834. Took stage to Boston

this morning to meet the Prudential Committee of the A. B. C. F. M. and report. All were surprised to see us, as nothing had been heard from us from the day of our embarkation in New York until we entered the rooms of the Board in Boston to-day. Our report was unfavorable to the present establishing of a mission in Patagonia.

CHAPTER XIV.

MR. DARWIN'S EXPLORATIONS AND EXPERIENCES.

Hilo, Hawaii, Dec. 1, 1876. Since our visit to Patagonia I have been much interested in several recent accounts of visitors to that savage land, as also to Tierra del Fuego and the Falkland Islands.

From the published journals of some of these intelligent and observant travellers I take the liberty to make some extracts which will be of interest to readers.

The distinguished naturalist Charles Darwin, in his "Voyage Round the World" in H.M.S. Beagle, under the command of Captain Fitz Roy, R.N., during the years 1832–1836, visited the Falkland Islands, North and Eastern Patagonia, the Strait of Magellan, Tierra del Fuego, and the western shores of Patagonia. (See new edition, D. Appleton & Co., New York, 1873.) The Beagle visited the Rio Negro, a river on the northern boundary of Patagonia; also Port Desire, Port St. Julian, and Santa Cruz on the Atlantic coast, where our then young and enthusiastic scientist had great opportunities to examine the flora, the fauna, and the geology of that wild country.

On the northern boundaries he saw the Spanish settlements and numbers of the half-tamed Indians. The country is described as barren and uninviting. South of this he saw very few Indians, and everywhere the face of the country was comparatively level, dry, sandy, and sterile. His description of an expedition with three boats and twenty-five men, one hundred and forty miles up the river Santa Cruz to the foot-hills of the Cordilleras, and within sixty miles of the Pacific Ocean, is very interesting. But it is remarkable that in all this distance, and during an absence from the Beagle of twenty-one days, they met no Indians, though they occasionally saw their tracks and the tracks of their horses and dogs.

It seems that the Beagle was at Port Desire and Port St. Julian in December, 1833, and January, 1834, while we at the same time were travelling in the region of the Strait of Magellan, surrounded by large clans of savages.

A Spanish colony once attempted a settlement at Port Desire, where they built a fort and many dwelling-houses; but the sterility of the soil, the lack of rain and of water, together with the fierce hostility of the inhabitants, led the settlers to abandon the enterprise.

Another settlement was commenced far to the north at Port St. Joseph. On a Sunday every soul except two men of this little colony was massacred by the savages.

Since then a considerable colony was settled at Port Famine on the Strait of Magellan. All but one of this colony perished of starvation, and hence the name which commemorates the painful tale of suffering. Connected with this sad history is the story of a visitation of the small-pox, which cut off many of the settlers. During this scourge the savages came to the colony and gathered up old waste papers which had been thrown away, and these papers conveyed the disease to them, so that a large number died. This fact filled them with fear of books and papers, and this, as I have been assured, was the reason why they were so disturbed by our writing and reading. And this may also help to explain another phenomenon which at the time was a mystery to us, viz., the rush of the savages and the circle formed around our tent in the night. This circle, I have been told, was the death-ring. It signifies the capture of a prisoner or prisoners. Then comes the consultation, and the decision for life or for death. If the former, the ring breaks up and the enclosed live; if the latter, death follows.

Mr. Darwin says, regarding the geology of Patagonia: " Differently from Europe, where the tertiary formations appear to have accumulated in bays, here along hundreds of miles of coast we have one great deposit, including many tertiary shells, all apparently extinct. The most common shell is a massive gigantic oyster, sometimes over a foot in diameter. These beds are covered by others of a peculiar white stone including much gypsum, and resembling chalk, but really of a pumiceous nature. It is highly remarkable from being composed, to at least one third part of its bulk, of infusoria. Professor Ehrenberg has already ascertained in it thirty oceanic forms.

"This bed extends for 500 miles along the coast, and probably for a considerably greater distance. At Port St. Julian its thickness is more than 800 feet. These white beds are everywhere capped by a mass of gravel, forming probably one of the largest beds of shingle in the world; it certainly extends from near the Rio Colorado to between 600 and 700 nautical miles southward; at Santa Cruz (a river a little south of St. Julian) it reaches to the foot of the Cordilleras; half way up the river its thickness is more than 200 feet; it probably everywhere extends to this great chain, whence the well-rounded pebbles of porphyry have been derived; we may consider its average breadth as 200 miles, and its average thickness as about 50 feet.

"When we consider that all these pebbles, countless as the grains of sand in the desert, have been derived from the slow falling of masses of rock on the old coast lines and banks of rivers; and that these fragments have been dashed into smaller pieces, and that each of them has been slowly rolled, rounded, and far transported, the mind is stupefied in thinking over the long, absolutely necessary lapse of years. Yet all this gravel has been transported, and probably rounded, subsequently to the deposition of the white beds, and long subsequently to the underlying beds with the tertiary shells.

"Everything in this southern continent has been effected on a grand scale: the land, from the Rio Plata to Tierra del Fuego, a distance of 1200 miles, has been raised in mass (and in Patagonia to a height of between 300 and 400 feet) within the period of the now existing sea-shells.

"The old and weathered shells left on the surface of the upraised plain still partially retain their colors. The uprising movement has been interrupted by at least eight long periods of rest, during which the sea ate deeply back into the land, forming at successive levels the long lines of cliffs or escarpments which separate the different plains as they rise like steps one behind the other. The elevatory movements and the eating-back power of the sea during the periods of rest have been equable over long lines of coast; for I was astonished to find that the step-like plains stand at nearly corresponding heights at far distant points. The lowest plain is 90 feet; high, and the highest which I ascended near the coast is 950 feet; and of this only relics are left in the form of flat gravel-capped hills. The upper plain of Santa Cruz slopes up to a height of 3000 feet at the foot of the Cordilleras. I have said that within the period of existing sea-shells Patagonia has been upraised 300 to 400 feet. I may add that within the period when icebergs transported boulders over the upper plain of Santa Cruz, the elevation has been at least 1500 feet.

Nor has Patagonia been affected only by upward movements: the extensive tertiary shells from Port St. Julian and Santa Cruz cannot have lived, according to Prof. E. Forbes, in a greater depth of water than from 40 to 250 feet; but they are now covered with a sea-deposited strata from 800 to 1000 feet in thickness: hence the bed of the sea on which these shells once lived must have sunk downwards several hundred feet to allow of the accumulation of the superincumbent strata. What a history of geological changes does the simply constructed coast of Patagonia reveal!"

In Appletons' Cyclopedia, under "Patagonia," will be found an interesting account of the survey of the river Santa Cruz and the lake Viedma, through which this river flows.

"The Santa Cruz, after the Negro by far the most important, as it is navigable throughout at all seasons, the depth being nowhere less than 9 feet, forms the eastern outlet of Lake Viedma (lat. 49° 30' S.), whence by a gentle curve S.E. it flows to its estuary, into which it discharges through a mouth three miles wide. The tide here rises 35 to 50 feet twice in the twenty-four hours.

Of the lakes existing in the interior, Viedma only is thoroughly known; it was explored in

October, 1874, by Lieutenant Feilberg, of the Argentine navy, who found it to be 27 miles long and 100 miles in circumference, with a western drainage to the Pacific, 32 miles distant. The explorer reached it by the Santa Cruz, and in his return decended the river (which has a current of 6 miles an hour) to Port Santa Cruz at the mouth in twenty six hours."

Passing over Professor Darwin's interesting remarks on the Falkland Islands, I will quote briefly from his " Journal on Tierra del Fuego."

"In the afternoon we anchored in the Bay of Good Success. While entering we were saluted in a manner becoming the inhabitants of this savage land. A group of Fuegians, partly concealed by the entangled forest, were perched on a wild point overhanging the sea; and as we passed by, they sprang up and, waving their tattered cloaks, sent forth a loud and sonorous shout. The savages followed the ship, and just before dark we saw their fire and again heard their wild cry. . . .

"In the morning the captain sent a party to communicate with the Fuegians. . . . When we were on shore the party looked rather alarmed, but continued talking and making gestures with great rapidity. It was without exception the most curious and interesting spectacle I ever beheld: I could not have believed how wide was the difference between savage and civilized man. . . . The party altogether closely resembled the devils which come on the stage in plays like *Der Freischütz*. Their very attitudes were abject, and the expression of their countenances distrustful, surprised, and startled. . . .

" During the former voyage of the Adventure and Beagle in 1826 to 1830, Captain Fitz Roy seized on a party of natives as hostages for the loss of a boat, which had been stolen to the great jeopardy of a party employed on the survey; and some of the natives as well as a child whom he bought for a pearl-button, he took with him to England, determining to educate them and instruct them in religion at his own expense. To settle these natives in their own country was one of the chief inducements to Captain Fitz Roy to undertake our present voyage; and before the Admiralty had resolved to send out this expedition, Captain Fitz Roy had generously chartered a vessel, and would himself have taken them back. The natives were accompanied by a missionary, R. Matthews, of whom and of the natives Captain Fitz Roy has published a full and excellent account. Two men, one of whom died in England of the small-pox, a boy and a little girl were originally taken; and we had now on board York Minster, Jemmy Button (whose name expresses his purchase-money) and Fuegia Basket."

Here Professor Darwin gives a lively sketch of the personal appearance and characteristics of the three Fuegians, after which he relates the efforts made by Captain Fitz Roy to find their friends and relatives, and to leave them in their native land. The mother and brothers of Jemmy were, after a long cruise, found in a little place called Woollya on the shore of Ponsonby Sound, among the mountains of Southern Fuego, and here he and York Minster and the girl Fuegia Basket were all left.

Touching this subject the Journal says: "Captain Fitz Roy having resolved to settle the Fuegians, according to their wishes, in Ponsonby Sound, four boats were equipped to carry them through the Beagle Channel. This channel, which was discovered by Captain Fitz Roy during the last voyage, is a most remarkable feature in the geography of this or indeed of any other country; it may be compared to the valley of Lochness, in

Scotland, with its chain of lakes and friths. It is about 120 miles long, with an average breadth, not subject to any very great variation, of about two miles; and is throughout the greater part so perfectly straight that the view, bounded on each side by a line of mountains, gradually becomes indistinct in the long distance. It crosses the southern part of Tierra del Fuego in an east and west line, and in the middle is joined at right angles on the south side by an irregular channel, which has been called Ponsonby Sound. This is the residence of Jemmy Button's tribe and family."

This little fleet of four boats with twenty-eight men, headed by Captain Fitz Roy, left the Beagle on the 19th of January, 1833, and arrived at Woollya on the 23d of January. On their way through Beagle Channel Professor Darwin remarks: " As we proceeded the scenery assumed a peculiar and very magnificent character. The mountains were here about 3000 feet high, and terminated in sharp and jagged points. They rose in one unbroken sweep from the water's edge, and were covered to the height of 1400 or 1500 feet by the dusky-colored forest. . . .

" At night we slept close to the junction of

Ponsonby Sound with the Beagle Channel. A small family of Fuegians who were living in the cove soon joined our party round a blazing fire. We were well clothed, and though sitting close to the fire were far from too warm; yet these naked savages, though further off, were observed, to our surprise, to be steaming with perspiration at undergoing such a roasting.

"During the night the news had spread, and early in the morning (23d) a fresh party arrived, belonging to the Tekenika, or Jemmy's tribe. Several of them had run so fast that their noses were bleeding; and their mouths frothed from the rapidity with which they talked; and with their naked bodies all bedaubed with black, white, and red, they looked like so many demoniacs who had been fighting.

"We then proceeded (accompanied by twelve canoes, each holding four or five people) down Ponsonby Sound to the spot where poor Jemmy expected to find his mother and relatives. . . . We found here a family of Jemmy's tribe, but not his relations; we made friends with them, and in the evening they sent a canoe to inform Jemmy's mother and brothers. The cove was bordered by some acres of good, sloping land not covered, as elsewhere, either by peat or by forest-trees . . . and as the spot was singularly favorable, Captain Fitz Roy determined to settle here the whole party, including Matthews, the missionary. Five days were spent in building for them three large wigwams, in landing their goods, in digging two gardens, and in sowing seeds. The next morning after our arrival the Fuegians began to pour in, and Jemmy's mother and brother arrived.

"The meeting was less interesting than that between a horse turned out into a field when he joins an old companion. There was no demonstration of affection; they simply stared for a short time at each other, and the mother immediately went to look after her canoe. . . .

" The women took much notice of and were very kind to Fuegia. We had already perceived that Jemmy had almost forgotten his own language.

" It was laughable, but almost pitiable, to hear him speak to his wild brother in English, and then ask him in Spanish, " No sabe ?" whether he did not understand. Everything went on peaceably during the three next days, whilst the gardens were digging and the wigwams building. Suddenly, however, on the 27th every woman and child disappeared. We were all uneasy at this, as neither York nor Jemmy could make out the cause. It was thought by some that they had been frightened by our cleaning and firing off our muskets on the previous evening; by others that it was owing to offence taken by an old savage who, when told to keep further off, had coolly spit in the sentry's face, and had then, by gestures acted over a sleeping Fuegian, plainly showed, as it was said, that he should like to cut up and eat our man.

"Captain Fitz Roy, to avoid the chance of an encounter, which would have been fatal to so many of the Fuegians, thought it advisable for us to sleep at a cove a few miles distant.

"Matthews, with his usual quiet fortitude, determined to stay with the Fuegians, and so we left them to pass their first awful night. On our return in the morning (28th) we were delighted to find all quiet. . . . Captain Fitz Roy determined to send the yawl and one whaleboat back to the ship, and to proceed with the other two boats to survey the western parts of the Beagle Channel, and afterwards to return and visit the settlement.

"*Feb.* 6. We arrived at Woollya. Matthews gave

so bad an account of the conduct of the Fuegians that Captain Fitz Roy determined to take him back to the Beagle ; and ultimately he was left at New Zealand, where his brother was a missionary. From the time of our leaving a regular system of plunder commenced—York and Jemmy lost many things, and Matthews almost everything which had not been concealed underground. He described the watch he was obliged to keep as most harassing. One day an old man whom Matthews asked to leave his wigwam immediately returned with a large stone in his hand. Another day a whole party came armed with stones and stakes, and some of the younger men and Jemmy's brother were crying. Matthews met them with presents. Another party showed by signs that they wished to strip him naked and pluck all the hairs out of his face and body. I think we arrived just in time to save his life. . . . It was melancholy leaving the three Fuegians with their savage countrymen, but it was a great comfort that they had no personal fears.

"On the 5th of March, 1834, we anchored in the cove at Woollya, but we saw not a soul there. We were alarmed at this, for the natives in Ponsonby Sound showed by gestures that there had been fighting, and we afterwards heard that the dreaded Oens men had made a descent. Soon a canoe, with a little flag flying, was seen approaching, with one of the men in it washing the paint off his face. This man was poor Jemmy, now a thin, haggard savage, with long disordered hair, and naked except a bit of blanket round his waist. We did not recognize him until he was close to us; for he was ashamed of himself, and turned his back to the ship. We had left him plump, fat, clean, and well dressed; I never saw so complete and grievous a change. As soon, however, as he was clothed, and the first flurry was over, things wore a good appearance. He dined with Captain Fitz Roy, and ate his dinner as tidily as formerly. He told us he had 'too much' (meaning enough) to eat, that he was not cold, that his relations were very good people, and that he did not wish to go back to England. In the evening we found out the cause of this great change in Jemmy's feelings, in the arrival of his young and nice-looking wife. He brought two beautiful otter-skins, and some spear-heads and arrows made with his own hands, for the captain. He said he had built a canoe for himself, and he boasted that he could talk a little of his own language. But it is a singular fact that he appears to have taught all his tribe some English. An old man spontaneously announced " Jemmy Button's wife." Jemmy had lost all his property. He told us that York Minster had built a large canoe, and with his wife Fuegia had several months since gone to his own country, and had taken farewell by an act of consummate villainy; he persuaded Jemmy and his mother to come with him, and then on the way deserted them by night, stealing every article of their property.

"Jemmy remained on board till the ship got under weigh, which frightened his wife, who continued crying violently till he got into his canoe. He returned loaded with valuable property. Every soul on board was sorry to shake hands with him for the last time.

"Every one must sincerely hope that Captain Fitz Roy's noble hope may be fulfilled, of being rewarded for the many generous sacrifices which he made for these Fuegians, by some shipwrecked sailors being protected by the descendants of Jemmy Button and his tribe. When Jemmy reached the shore he lighted a signal-fire, and the smoke curled up, bidding a last and long farewell, as the ship stood on her course into the open sea."

Who will not admire the generous, patient, and persistent efforts of Captain Fitz Roy in trying to plant the germs of Christianity and civilization in the heart of the wild, dreary, and savage land of Tierra del Fuego? And who will not mourn that he felt compelled by the feelings of humanity to remove the missionary Matthews from scenes so sickening and dangers so appalling as were met among these wretched savages?

Professor Darwin thinks he has sufficient proof from the testimony of Captain Low, a sealing-master, from Jemmy Button and others, that the Fuegians are cannibals. He says, "The different tribes, when at war, are cannibals. It is certainly true that, when pressed in winter by hunger, they kill and devour their old women before they kill their dogs. The boy being asked by Mr. Low why they did this, answered, 'Doggies catch otters; old women no.' This boy described the way in which they are killed by being held over smoke, and thus choked. He imitated their screams as a joke, and described the parts of their bodies which are considered best to eat."

CHAPTER XV.

THE CAPTIVE IN PATAGONIA.

FOR further information in regard to the savages of Eastern Patagonia and along the Strait of Magellan, I refer the reader to "The Captive in Patagonia; or, A Personal Narrative of the Capture, Sufferings, and Escape of Benjamin Franklin Bourne, Mate of the Schooner John Allyne, of New Bedford," published by Gould & Lincoln, Boston, 1853.

This schooner, A. Brownwell, master, sailed from New Bedford on the 13th February, 1849, bound to California in search of gold. In passing through the Strait of Magellan the vessel anchored on the 1st of May within the eastern part of the Strait, and very near the place where the Mary Jane left Mr. Arms and myself, and evidently among the same tribe of savages with whom we sojourned in 1833-4.

Mr. Bourne was sent on shore to trade with the natives, but through the disobedienee of his boat's crew he fell into the hands of the savages, who supposed him to be the master of the schooner, and who retained him doubtless with the hope of securing a large ransom for his delivery. Unfortunately all efforts to secure his release failed; the John Allyne sailed without him; he was carried to the Indians' camp in the country, and a feeling of horror, almost of despair, such as cannot be known but by experience, came over him.

The Chilian Government at that time had a penal settlement at Port Famine, sixty or seventy miles westward in the Strait. To this place Mr. Bourne begged earnestly and repeatedly to be taken, but his plea was rejected. In his agony for escape he sometimes became desperate, using flattery and threatening, promising his captors rich gifts when they should restore him to freedom, and threatening exemplary vengeance on any one who should dare to hurt him. For all this duplicity he apologizes, as it seemed to him necessary on account of his desperate condition.

Mr. Bourne mentions horrid murders committed while he was in exile; he also thinks that cannibalism was practised in Patagonia, but with great secrecy. He records two cases where he was surrounded with what he calls "the fatal ring," where his life was in great peril, and where he mercifully escaped through the intervention of his guardian chief, who pleaded that his life might be spared until they had obtained the promised presents.

After three months and seven days of physical sufferings and perils, and of mental anguish that can never be told, he succeeded in persuading the Indians to go as far north as Port Santa Cruz, where there was a small islet which the savages called Holland. At this island lay a vessel with a few men come thither to collect guano.

Bourne set a signal on the shore for a boat to come from the island; but it was not until the second day that any movement was made in response. At length, however, a boat approached the shore and was hailed, but refused to land for fear of the savages. Mr. Hall, who headed the boat, told Bourne to dive into the sea and swim off, promising to care for him when once on board.

But how could he disentangle himself from the Indians, who kept close to him with their knives, determined not to let him go until they received the rewards promised? To the poor captive it was a case of life or death. The savages ordered him to go back to their camp. He signified that he would by and by. They watched him. Suddenly he darted from them and plunged into the roaring surf. They followed with drawn knives, but the surf stopped them, and he by a desperate struggle reached the boat, and was taken exhausted and chilled to the island.

This was on the 7th of August, 1849, and in the dead of winter. He was taken captive on the first of May, making his captivity ninety-nine days. He had no further communication with the Patagonians, and all their hopes of rewards were blasted. This narrative of Mr. Bourne is painfully interesting, and it will well repay the reader. His descriptions of life and manners in Patagonia are graphic and life-like, and more correct than the stories of some who have written on that country.

CHAPTER XVI.

"THE STORY OF CAPTAIN ALLEN FRANCIS GARDINER, R.N."

I NOW propose to add a few facts bearing on the subject of Patagonia and Tierra del Fuego taken from a very interesting little volume prepared by J. W. Marsh, M.A., and W. H. Stirling, B.A. (London, 1867), with the above title.

Having an earnest desire for the evangelization of the heathen, Captain Gardiner relinquished the naval service and devoted his life to missionary work. He was three years in the Zulu country in South Africa, exploring and establishing a missionary station at Port Natal.

"A few years later he attempted to obtain entrance into New Guinea. He went from island to island of the Indian Archipelago, and from governor to magistrate, but all his efforts were baffled." He then turned his attention to South America, exploring extensively both among the Spanish states and the aboriginal tribes. He made an earnest effort to establish a Christian mission among the unconquered Araucanians on the south of Chili; but here he was foiled by the opposition; as he believed, of the Spanish priests.

In 1841 Captain Gardiner attempted to organize an expedition from the island of Chiloe to travel eastward, cross a pass in the Cordilleras, and to communicate with the natives residing on the eastern side. This plan also failed, and he returned to Valparaiso, whence he sailed for the Falkland Islands, and arrived at Port Louis in Berkley Sound December 23d, 1841. These islands he now selected as the base of missionary operations, purposing to bring over a few of the Fuegians or Patagonians to the islands to be instructed in English, and also to assist the missionaries in acquiring the language of the Patagonians. The seat of government was then at Port Louis, but it was afterwards established at Port William, where the town of Stanley has since been built, and where the English have planted a small colony.

In March, 1842, Captain Gardiner entered the Strait of Magellan in a schooner, and made an attempt to persuade some of the Fuegians on the south side of the Strait to go with him to the

Falklands. Failing in this, he went over to the north shore and anchored in Gregory Bay, where we first landed. Finding no Indians here, he proceeded westward twelve miles to Oazy Harbor, where he found a clan headed by a chief called Wissale, with whom he made an engagement to establish a mission to be under the protection of this chief. He then returned with his family to England, made efforts to interest Christians in the South American enterprise, and brought out a Mr. Hunt to labor with the tribe just named. This was in February, 1845. Captain Gardiner found all things changed. Most of the tribe were absent; they were also divided, and Wissale was sullen and unfriendly.

So this effort failed, and Captain Gardiner and Mr. Hunt returned to England. In due time Captain Gardiner came back with a Mr. Gonzales, a Spanish Protestant, to South America, where he travelled heroically to find aboriginal tribes to whom the Gospel could be preached. He finally settled Gonzales in Bolivia, and in February, 1846, we find him again in England, full of zeal in his South American enterprise.

But he had not yet given up his purpose to make another effort for Tierra del Fuego. He travelled and lectured in England and Scotland, but with small pecuniary success. For want of money he proposed to the committee to take a one-decked boat, a dingey, a whaleboat, two small wigwams, four sailors, and one ship-carpenter, and sail for Staten Island, which lies due east from Tierra del Fuego. All things ready, they sailed in the bark Clymene, bound to Peru, on the 7th of January, 1848. On the 15th of March they made Staten Island, and from this time till the first of April they struggled hard and with incredible suffering to establish a station on Picton Island, at Banner Cove; but being thwarted by the thieving habits of the savages, they sailed for Payta in Peru.

From Peru the indefatigable Captain Gardiner returned again to England, with irrepressible zeal urging the Patagonian Missionary Society to go forward, and striving, almost against hope, to collect funds for the purpose. Mr. Ritchie, the honorable secretary of the society, had resigned and gone to Liverpool, and no member of the committee was willing to take his place. At length Captain Gardiner persuaded the Rev. Geo. Packenham Despard to come to the rescue.

Again he travelled over England and Scotland

in search of funds, but with little success, until a generous lady gave him £700, and afterwards £300 more. Two launches 26 by 8½ feet were purchased, and two small tenders, and provisions for six months.

Mr. Williams (surgeon), Mr. Maidment, Joseph Erwin, and three Cornish fishermen—viz., John Pearce, John Badcock, and John Bryant—were appointed to go to Tierra del Fuego on this expedition. With this party Captain Gardiner sailed from Liverpool in the bark Ocean Queen, bound for San Francisco, on the 7th of September, 1850, and on the 5th of the following December arrived at Picton Island, and the Ocean Queen anchored in Banner Cove. Hence he writes: "On Friday, the 6th, we erected our tents, and slept on shore. On the 7th we constructed a strong fence of trunks of trees, etc., round our position, leaving only one small opening. This night and during Sunday the number of natives increased. . . . Their rudeness and pertinacious endeavor to force a way into the tents, and to purloin our things, at length became so systematic and resolute that it was not possible to retain our position without resorting to force, from which, of course, we refrained. For the present we must keep the stores and everything in the boats. As soon as the Ocean Queen leaves us I purpose going to Button Island and endeavoring to find out Jemmy, in the hope of persuading him or some of his relatives to locate here."

The Ocean Queen sailed on the 19th of December. An attempt was then made to go to Woollya in search of Jemmy Button, but in this their two small boats and one launch were lost. They were in distress, and the expedition to Woollya failed.

On the 2d of February, 1851, Mr. Williams writes: "How evident that we were not in a position to commence, with such slight means, so arduous an undertaking! We are now all agreed that nothing short of a brigantine or schooner of eighty or a hundred tons can answer our ends, and to procure this ultimately the captain has fully determined to use every effort. A short acquaintance with the natives confirmed the unfavorable reports which such writers as Fitz Roy, King, and Darwin had given."

Fearing the savages at Banner Cove, the whole company had removed to Spaniard Harbor, where they watched for the arrival of a vessel to bring them supplies of provisions that never came.

They made one more trip to Banner Cove, on Picton Island, to bring away provisions they had concealed, and to leave notices to show where they were gone, in case of any vessel searching for them in Banner Cove.

The provisions of the missionaries were getting reduced day by day, their powder and shot were being exhausted, their fishing-net gave out; Mr. Williams and Mr. Badcock were sick; the scurvy began to attack some of their number; no vessel appeared for their relief, and their condition was truly forlorn.

In view of death by starvation, nothing but the all-sufficient grace of God, in hope of eternal life, sustained them. But faith anchored their souls to the "Rock of Ages."

On the night of the 28th of July, 1851, Mr. Badcock departed in triumph to his heavenly home. He had suffered with fears that he was not accepted by the Beloved; but all these clouds of doubt fled away before the visions of a strong faith, and just before he expired he sang with a loud voice:

> "Arise, my soul, arise,
>   Shake off thy guilty fears ;
>   The bleeding Sacrifice
>   In my behalf appears.
>   Before the throne my Surety stands,
>   My name is written on His hands."

A part of the company slept in the Speedwell, their only remaining boat, and the other part occupied a cavern about one mile and a half distant on the shore. On the rocks at the entrance of this cave were afterwards found the words of the 62d Psalm, verses 5-8, painted with this date, July 5th, 1851.

On the 25th of August Joseph Erwin went to his rest, deeply lamented. Captain Gardiner writes of him, "Twice has he accompanied me to Tierra del Fuego, and on all occasions proved himself worthy of my highest confidence and esteem." John Bryant died on the 27th of August. Maidment labored to the end of life to help and comfort his sick and dying comrades. " On September 2d he left the boat, but was unable to return, and his remains were found in Pioneer Cavern."

Captain Gardiner was fast growing weaker and weaker. On the 27th August he wrote his last letter of affectionate counsel to his son ; on the

28th he wrote a tender farewell to his daughter; and on the 29th he penned his final letter to his beloved wife. I quote a brief extract: "I am passing through the furnace, but blessed be my heavenly Shepherd, He is with me, and I shall not want. He has kept me in perfect peace, and my soul rests and waits on Him only. . . . I trust poor Fuegia and South America will not be abandoned."

On the 30th he made an unsuccessful effort to join the suffering party at Cook's River, the place where the launch was anchored. On the 2d of September we find this entry in his diary: "Hope deferred, not lost." His last entry in his journal is on September 5th. On the 6th he wrote his last words in a note to Mr. Williams:

"MY DEAR MR. WILLIAMS:

"The Lord has seen fit to call home another of our little company. Our dear departed brother left the boat on Tuesday at noon, and has not since returned; doubtless he is in the presence of his Redeemer whom he served so faithfully. Yet a little while, and through grace we may join that blessed throng to sing the praises of Christ throughout eternity. I neither hunger nor thirst, though five days without food! Marvellous loving-kindness to me a sinner!

"Your affectionate brother in Christ,
"ALLEN F. GARDINER."

The sad narrative tells us that on the 22d of October, 1851, the schooner John Davison, sent from Montevideo by Mr. Lafone to look after this missionary party, anchored in Banner Cove, where the master, Captain Smyley, read the directions of Captain Gardiner painted on the rocks, "Gone to Spaniard Harbor," dug up the buried bottles, read the enclosed letters, and ran to Spaniard Harbor. Here he found one dead body in the boat, another on the beach, and one buried. These he supposed to be Pearce, Williams, and Badcock. "The sight," says Captain Smyley, "was awful in the extreme. The two captains who went with me in the boat cried like children. Books, papers, medicine, clothing, and tools were strewed along the beach and on the boat's deck and cuddy."

A gale coming on, Captain Smyley was driven out to sea with only time to bury the corpses without making further search.

On the 19th of January, 1852, H.M.S. Dido,

Captain Morshead, arrived at Banner Cove from the Falkland Islands. The bottles and letters were gone, but the notice on the rocks remained, and directed the ship to Spaniard Harbor. Here they found the bodies of Captain Gardiner and Mr. Maidment.

Captain Morshead writes: " On one of the papers was written, ' If you will walk along the beach for a mile and a half you will find us in the other boat, hauled up in the mouth of a river at the head of the harbor on the south side. Delay not, we are starving.' At this sad intelligence it was impossible to leave that night, though the weather looked very threatening. I landed the next morning, January 2d, and went to the head of the harbor with Lieutenant Gaussen, Mr. Roberts, and Mr. Evans. We found there the wreck of a boat with part of her gear and stores, with quantities of clothing, with the remains of two bodies which I conclude to be Mr. Williams (surgeon) and John Pearce. . . . Their remains were collected together, and buried close to the spot, and the funeral service read by Lieutenant Underwood, and three volleys of musketry were the only tribute I could pay to this loftyminded man and his devoted companions, . . .

and before noon the Dido was proceeding safely on her voyage."

When the tidings of this mournful calamity reached England sceptics censured and scoffers scoffed, and the friends of Patagonia mourned over crushed hopes. But they were soon reassured by the bold and unconquered zeal of Mr. Despard, the secretary, who published widely his determination that "with the help of God, the mission shall be maintained."

The bugle-blast aroused the friends of missions to renewed efforts, and in 1854 a schooner named Allen Gardiner was launched at Dartmouth, and sailed from Bristol with a newly appointed company of missionaries to establish a station on the Falkland Islands, to which some Fuegians might be brought for instruction in English, and from whom the missionaries might learn the Fuegian tongue.

The Allen Gardiner sailed on the 24th of October, 1854, under the command of Captain Parker Snow, with Mr. G. Phillips as catechist and Mr. Ellis as surgeon, for Keppel Island near West Falkland, where the station was established on the 5th of February, 1855.

The Allen Gardiner soon made a voyage to

Tierra del Fuego, where Jemmy Button was found living with his family.

On the 2d of June, 1856, Secretary Despard sailed from Plymouth for the Falkland Islands as superintendent of the mission. He was accompanied by the Rev. J. F. Ogle, M.A, Mr. Allen W. Gardiner, son of the lamented Captain Gardiner; by Mr. C. Turpin and Mr. W. Bartlett, as missionaries and helpers. They arrived August 30th.

Secretary Despard soon made a trip to Patagonia in the Allen Gardiner, and also to Tierra del Fuego, where young Gardiner visited the grave of his devoted father and the awful mementoes of the deaths of that forlorn hope of soldiers of the cross. In June, 1858, Mr. Gardiner visited Tierra del Fuego again with Mr. Turpin. They went to Woollya, found Jemmy Button and his wife with three children, and they all went to the Falklands to spend six months with the missionaries. They were overjoyed to see this Fuegian family, and on hearing that they were on board the Allen Gardiner as she came into Keppel Island harbor, Mrs. Despard writes, "then arose a shout of joy and praise among us."

Jemmy and family remained with the missionaries until November, when Mr. Despard took them back to Woollya in the Allen Gardiner, on which occasion Mrs. Despard writes: "My husband left us on the 16th, accompanied by Messrs. Phillips and Turpin and the Button family for Tierra del Fuego. I cannot tell you how we miss our late guests. During their stay here they behaved extremely well, never doing anything to offend or annoy us. As to Jemmy, his politeness was extreme, and I ever found him most grateful. For any little trifle I gave him he would go and pick me a beautiful bouquet of wild flowers or spear me some fish. He was always clean. He quickly recovered his English, and understood us better than we understood him. He knows that there is a God who has created all things. He also knows about our blessed Saviour."

Did not Admiral Fitz Roy rejoice to hear this, and feel that his generous efforts to educate this dark heathen boy were not in vain?

Mr. Despard with two catechists remained a month at Woollya with the Button family, built a house in English style for them, and then returned to the Falkland station with three Fuegians and their wives, two boys, and a little child.

Under date of October 4th, 1859, Mr. Despard

writes: "These Fuegians are just returning to their own home.... They are greatly changed in manners. The two lads Lucca-enges and Okokko-enges are quite polite. 'If you please,' 'Thank you,' 'Good-morning' are ever heard in the right time and place. They give thanks at their meals, and pray at their bedside.... The men are also much improved—coming to daily worship, and generally twice on Sunday. They are now decent in their habits, tidily dressed, and as far as our imperfect medium of communication goes they have been taught the knowledge of God."

On the 6th of October these nine Fuegian were put on board the Allen Gardiner, under the charge of Mr. Phillips, to be returned to Woollya with specific instructions from Superintendent Despard to Mr. Phillips.

After the time for the return of the vessel from Fuegia had passed Mr. Despard and the missionaries became anxious for her safety, and Mr. Despard went to Stanley and despatched the schooner Nancy, Captain Smyley, to Woollya. Captain Smyley returned with these heart-rending tidings: "Mr. Phillips, Captain Fell, the two mates of the schooner, and four seamen have all been massacred by the natives in Woollya, and the schooner plundered." The news was awful, and the missionaries were stunned with amazement. They groaned and wept and prayed. They wept and prayed for the crushed widows, the mothers and fathers and children of the murdered, and for the poor, deluded, wretched savages of Fuego, whose cupidity and brutality had led them to imbrue their hands in the blood of those who had come to seek and to save them.

The following are the facts in brief of this terrible massacre. The Allen Gardiner arrived at Woollya November 1st, and the missionaries held friendly intercourse with the natives for several days. Meanwhile many canoes arrived from neighboring islands, but no harm was suspected. On Sunday, the 6th, all hands except the cook came on shore for public worship. While engaged in divine service the savages fell upon them and slaughtered the whole company. The cook, on seeing from the deck the awful work on shore, escaped around a point in a boat, and hid in the woods, until hunger and cold compelled him to reveal himself to the natives, who stripped and plundered him but spared his life. He was afterwards taken into the Button family and well treated until Captain Smyley arrived and took him on board the Nancy.

Captain Smyley went a second time to Woollya and brought away the wreck of the Allen Gardiner, which had not been burned. On this occasion Okokko begged to be taken back to Keppel Island with his wife Camilenna, and for a long time they were the only Fuegian residents on the Falklands.

Mr. and Mrs. Despard returned to England early in 1862, leaving the farm and property under the care of Mr. Bartlett, and the natives under the charge of Mr. Bridges.

On reaching England, the Allen Gardiner was repaired and increased in length and efficiency, and in August of the same year she returned to the South Atlantic with a new reinforcement of missionaries, and with Mr. Sterling as superintendent. They spent three weeks in the River Plata, while Mr. Sterling visited Montevideo and Buenos Ayres on missionary business. Thence they sailed for the Falklands, touching at the Rio Negro and Santa Cruz in Patagonia, and arriving at Keppel Island on the 30th of January, 1863. Only two adult Fuegians, Okokko and wife, and their two little children remained.

It was now determined to reopen communication with Tierra del Fuego, as all intercourse with those savage tribes had ceased since the massacre in 1859. So taking on board the tamed Okokko, the Allen Gardiner sailed once more for Fuego in March, touching at Banner Cove, Packsaddle Bay, and Woollya. Through the agency of Okokko the natives became friendly. He went on shore with his wife and children at Woollya, and spent a Sabbath in speaking to the people, numbers of whom were desirous to go to Keppel Island. Seven new natives were taken, making with the Okokkos eleven in all. Soon after this three Patagonian Indians were brought over from Santa Cruz, where a mission station had been commenced.

In February, 1864, the Allen Gardiner sailed again for Tierra del Fuego, taking the Okokko family to settle them in Woollya, where he and his wife were to act as Christian teachers. Touching at Wollaston Island and other places on the way, and having communication with the natives, they reached Woollya on the 7th of March. Here they learned that a malignant sickness had swept off a large number of the people of all ages, and that Jemmy Button and many of his kindred were dead, and there was great mourning among the survivors.

On this visit the place was found where the bodies of the massacred company were buried under a large heap of stones. The funeral service was read over the rocky tomb, while the flag of the schooner hung at half mast and the ship's company bowed their heads in sorrow.

This mournful yet successful visit to Woollya ended on the 21st of March, and they returned to the Falklands, On a subsequent visit it was found that Okokko's house, goats, and all his property had been destroyed by natives, and that his life had been threatened because he told the people of God, whom they could not see, and of a hell where the wicked would be punished.

In view of this outburst of insane violence Okokko was much distressed, and it was determined that he and his family should return to the Falklands for further instruction. Another company of Fuegians, also, went over to attend the school at Keppel Island.

Again the Allen Gardiner sailed for England, having on board Mr. Stirling and four Fuegians. Early in the year 1867 she returned to the mission station on Keppel Island, taking back the four young Fuegians to the school established there, and this is the latest information I have been able to obtain of that heroic, that mournfully tragic, that patient and persistent effort to Christianize and to civilize the wretched inhabitants of Tierra del Fuego.

Those who have no sympathy with the command of Him who died to save our race, "Go ye into all the world and preach the gospel to every creature," may pity the weakness or sneer at the fanaticism of men who sacrificed life with all its comforts in an effort to save the abject savages of Tierra del Fuego; while others will admire their zeal, their patience, and their unconquerable faith, thus leaving them in the hands of Him in whose name they went forth among the gentiles with the assurance that "their record is on high."

CHAPTER XVII.

LATER EFFORTS FOR PATAGONIA.

LET us now return and take a rapid glance at Patagonia to see some of the things which under God our faithful English brethren have done for those benighted tribes since our sojourn among them :

" While the station on Keppel Island was being formed, voyages were also made to the coast of Patagonia every year. The wandering habits of the Patagonians, however, rendered visits to their coasts very unsatisfactory. . . . Mr. Schmid volunteered to go alone and travel with some one of the Patagonian tribes, hoping that in this way something might be done towards acquiring the language." *

There was then a Chilian penal settlement at Sandy Point near Port Famine. In March, 1859, Mr. Despard and Mr. Schmid visited this colony and made arrangements with the Chilian Gov-

* See "Story of Allen Gardiner," page 1.

ernor and an Indian chief that Mr. Schmid should travel into the interior under the guidance and protection of said chief, whose name was Ascaik, visiting the roaming clans, becoming acquainted with their habits of life, and learning their language. As a reward for this service, provided it were executed in good faith, Ascaik was to receive, on their return to Sandy Point, one barrel each of bread and flour, half a barrel of sugar, and a quantity of tobacco, with presents to all the Indians.

This contract being written and deposited with the Governor, Schmid set out with his Indian guide and his clan, travelling to the east along the Gregory hills, where Mr. Arms and I roamed, to the eastern entrance of Magellan Strait, where they found a wrecked bark, the Anne Baker, of Liverpool. Here the natives found intoxicants, got drunk, had an awful night, fought, killed two men, and wounded others.

This was an early experience of trouble. The clan then travelled northward and met a troop coming down from the vicinity of the Rio Negro. The Schmid party returned to the wreck after travelling six days, and here another drunken brawl occurred.

At length Schmid returned to Sandy Point; his chief, Ascaik, died suddenly; the Allen Gardiner had not arrived with his supplies and presents for the Indians (she was detained by the massacre and troubles at Tierra del Fuego); and finding an opportunity he sailed for Valparaiso, and thence to England.

In June, 1861, he came again with Mr. Hunziker to Sandy Point. With this fellow-laborer he set out under the guidance of Casimero and other Patagonians, and travelled eastward once more until they reached the main camp of the Indians at the river Gallegos.

Presents were given to the chiefs and they seemed pleased.

The missionaries then travelled from place to place with the Indians until late in the autumn, when they returned to the colony at Sandy Point, and soon took passage for the Falkland Islands to arrange for a permanent station somewhere in Patagonia. The roaming mission helped to acquire the language, but it failed to instruct the savages in the principles, duties, and privileges of Christianity and civilization. "Accordingly in May, 1862, the rudiments of a station were formed at Weddell's Bluff." This was ten miles within the entrance of the river Santa Cruz, in lat. 50° S.

Mr. Schmid and Mr. Hunziker occupied this station, but it was not till after about three months that they saw any Indians. Thus their residence was lonely and dreary, and the time seemed to be spent in vain.

Mr. Schmid resolved to travel south in search of natives. He journeyed wearily for sixteen days, and did not return until December, bringing with him only one Indian, an old acquaintance, Casimero, of Sandy Point. This chief promised that his tribe would visit Santa Cruz in two months. The brethren were greatly disheartened by their long solitude, but at length, after waiting eleven months for letters, the Allen Gardiner on her way from England to the Falklands came into port on the 1st of January, 1863. The vessel remained twenty-eight days in the Santa Cruz River, but during all that time no Indians appeared. During the following May the Allen Gardiner came again to this station, but no natives had yet arrived, and the missionaries were sad and discouraged. On the very next day, however, they were made glad by the arrival of a large clan. From Monday to Thursday it was estimated that four hundred had arrived from the south or from the Magellan Strait. These were led by the young chief Gemoki, son of Ascaik. With the chiefs of this tribe Mr. Stirling labored to secure the promise that they would favor a school for their children at Santa Cruz, leaving them with the missionaries, while the fathers hunted, and returning periodically to visit them, to bring them guanaco meat, robes, etc. But the chiefs were jealous of such teachings, offered many objections to the proposed plan, and would make no promises.

By travelling much among the Indians Mr. Schmid had gained considerable knowledge of their language. He had prepared a vocabulary in alphabetical order, and an outline of grammar, and he was able to converse with some facility in the Patagonian tongue. This was a great achievement, and a very essential step towards Christianizing the savages.

Mr. Hunziker also had made good progress in the same direction, while the missionaries of the southern tribes of Tierra del Fuego were fast mastering that strange and savage tongue through the help of their pupils on Keppel Island. Thus some of the greatest obstacles in the way of intelligent communication with the tribes were removed.

The Allen Gardiner, on her way out from England in December, 1862, visited the Rio Negro, and left two young missionaries at Patagones to study the Spanish and the Patagonian languages, with a view to establish a missionary base there in order to carry the Gospel to the tribes in the near vicinity and on the north, south, and west.

Patagones is a Spanish settlement, built on both sides of the Rio Negro, the north side being called El Carmen, and the south El Merced. It is said that for about half the year the Indians from all parts come to this settlement to trade. Even those that hunt along the Strait of Magellan often travel as far north as the Rio Grande to trade, or to steal horses, sheep, and horned cattle. It is also said that on one occasion the Indians made a raid and drove off 10,000 sheep from the ranch of one man not far from Patagones. Such forays embitter the Spaniards against the natives, and the Government of the Argentine Confederation keeps a guard of regular troops, supplemented by 200 or 300 tamed Indians, along the frontiers, to protect the settlements from the independent tribes.

In July, 1863, the superintendent of the Patagonian mission visited the Rio Negro again, and obtained a promise from the Government of Buenos Ayres, through the Minister of the Interior, of " all the moral support in its power."

At first a padre at Patagones opposed this mission earnestly, forbidding all the people under his influence to listen to the heretical English teachers or to read the Bible. But this priest sickened and died. In his last sickness he was attended by the Rev. George Humble, M.D., who commenced his missionary work at Patagones in October, 1864. The superintendent writes : " We are glad to record that for many months before the padre's decease there was a softening down of his hostility to the Protestant missionaries."

It has been remarked that the station at Santa Cruz was abandoned. Messrs. Schmid and Hunziker visited England and Germany, were married, and returned to their work in South America; the former being stationed at Bahia Blanca, in Buenos Ayres, and Mr. Hunziker with Dr. Humble at Patagones. From this Northern Patagonia mission I have been able to collect no information since August, 1865. It was then hopeful.

From the Fuegian mission my latest knowledge

is of January 25th, 1867. I trust its "winter is past, the rain over and gone, the flowers appearing, and the time of singing come." I long to hear the present state of these missions, and hope and pray that after such severe and repeated trials, such painful sufferings and sore disappointments, and after such undying patience, such unyielding faith, and such indomitable perseverance, the toils, the tears, the hunger, the bloody sacrifices, the prayers of agony, the "hopes deferred," and the love which cannot die, have all been rewarded.

I hope to hear that the "Light which is to lighten the gentiles," and which is to "enlighten every man," has penetrated the gloomy realms of Patagonia, and brought ' life and immortality" to the debased Fuegian. If the disciples of the "Man of Sorrows" are to "go into all the world," then surely they are to go into Patagonia ; and if the first great Missionary to this lost race did not withhold His " face from shame and spitting, or His soul from death," that He might save man from ruin, why then should His redeemed ones count their mortal lives dear to them in this terrible struggle with "the god of this world"? "The disciple is not above his Master," and to all the faithful the word of promise is, " In due season ye shall reap, if ye faint not."

It is true, as millions now in glory can testify, that "they who sow in tears shall reap in joy," and that "he who goeth forth and weepeth, bearing precious seed, shall doubtless come again with rejoicing, bringing his sheaves with him."

THE END.

www.ingramcontent.com/pod-product-compliance
Lightning Source LLC
Chambersburg PA
CBHW030729230426
43667CB00007B/654